Dreamland park c1922

Dreamland
Remembered

140 years of seaside fun in Margate

– Includes the Lido, Cliftonville

by NICK EVANS

Published independently

Contents

Introduction 4

The early days (1863-1920) 5

A time of prosperity (1920-1940) 14

Post war revival (1945-1968) 37

New brooms herald
a new era (1969-1981) 60

To the Millennium
– and beyond? (1981-2003) 73

A leisurely life
at the Lido (1920-2003) 85

Acknowledgements 112

Introduction

Youth was never properly misspent without visiting Dreamland at least a couple of times in adolescence. Many have fond memories of the famous Scenic Railway – for decades the centrepiece of the 20 acre amusement park – as well as rides including the Astroglide, the Big Wheel, the Caterpillar, the Dodgems, the Racing Coaster, the River Caves, the Waterchute and the Waltzer, and numerous sideshows clustered around the park.

An outing to Margate simply wasn't complete without spending time in Dreamland – indeed it was often the main reason for going to the East Kent resort every summer. Many will have descended on Dreamland from across the country either in a beanfeast coach outing, on the back of a scooter or as one of the family on a bucket and spade holiday.

Dreamland was designed to appeal across the age range but there was more than just the amusement park to enjoy. Cinemas, ballroom dancing, discos, bingo, summer shows, skating – ice and roller – and squash have all been part of the seafront scene over the years. Not far away in Cliftonville was the Lido pleasure centre, forming another main arm of the Iles empire which kept family control of both sites for five decades. There, thousands enjoyed the open air swimming pool, the variety of themed bars or for young women, the weekly beauty contests.

This book looks at both Dreamland and the Lido from their beginnings, their heydays immediately before and after World War Two as well as their falling from favour when society's expectations of leisure and holiday time changed.

Many of the photographs in this book formed the holding company's own publicity material handed on to my late father Bill Evans, who was Dreamland and the Lido's press officer from the early 1970s until the Bembom Brothers took over in 1981. Much of the history was also collected by Bill throughout this period.

Without his careful stewardship of this material, one can only guess at what might have otherwise happened to it. Other photographs and information have been supplied by Margate Museum, Kent County Library, Margate, and Mr Raymond Dolling.

There are many hundreds, if not thousands, of images of Dreamland and the Lido. For this reason the choices included in this book can only be a representative sample.

It is appropriate to acknowledge here the photographers hired by Margate Estates Ltd who captured the images in the first place, among them Edward Cox and Sunbeam Photos, as well as those taken by the Isle of Thanet Gazette.

I hope you will agree it is an impressive collection, acting now as a fine record of past times when holidays were spent on home shores – only the wealthy went abroad – the sun shone throughout the summer, the next ice cream was never far away and there was always a show or a movie to enjoy in the evening.

Nick Evans
Whitstable
August 2003

1. *This is the earliest known view of Spiers & Pond's Hall By The Sea which can be seen on the right and would have been taken during the late 1860s. The man standing fourth from left was the Hall's strongman who was hanged after murdering a prostitute in the gardens in 1895.*

The early days

Dreamland's origins can be traced back to 1863 when rival railway companies found themselves at loggerheads bringing trippers to Margate, a lucrative trade, for the town was a fast growing seaside resort.

The South Eastern Railway had opened its line to the town in 1846 from Ramsgate but now arch rival London, Chatham & Dover Railway was trying to muscle in on the act and break SER's monopoly.

Confident of winning parliamentary permission, LCDR built a terminus on the seafront right next door to SER's station, and even ran a test train there in May 1864. But the move meant the rivals' sets of tracks were interwoven and so the railway inspectorate refused to sanction the new development.

Undaunted, LCDR decided to build another station a short distance away calling it Margate West to serve passengers from London and Medway. Initially intended as a terminus, the company was given permission to continue the line to Ramsgate before the track was laid so plans were revised to make it a through station.

All this expensive railway wrangling saw a new building standing empty until 1867 when LCDR finally solved the problem by leasing it to its catering contractor Spiers & Pond.

The caterers christened the building The Hall By The Sea, opening it as a dance hall to satisfy the latest crazes of the lancers, the quadrille and the polka. Some 2,000 people could sachay to their heart's delight in what was one of the largest ballrooms in the country.

The manager, E P Hingston, and his successor Edward Murray, presented a variety of entertainments. Operatic and orchestral concerts were held and there were continual balls and dances, notably the annual Regatta Ball and fund raising nights for the Margate Surf Boat (predecessor of the life boat).

Inside, drapes were hung from the ceilings and walls, barely disguising its origins as a railway station. Despite these efforts, The Hall By The Sea was considered inferior to the long established and well-appointed Assembly Rooms in Cecil Square whose ideas it copied.

The Hall proved to be one of Spiers & Pond's less successful ventures – the company was better known as a pioneer of station buffets and refreshment cars – and by 1870 the decision was taken to pull out.

By now the passing of the Bank Holiday Act and Gladstone's 'Penny per Mile' rail legislation had started to see the lower middle and working classes coming in great numbers to the seaside. They wanted something more down-to-earth – dancing was not for them. The building was put up for auction but failed to find a buyer. Later though it was sold privately to Alderman Thomas Dalby Reeve, then Mayor of Margate, and a prosperous local businessman.

He paid £3,750 for the Hall, along with a non-commissioned railway embankment running from it, and nearby allotments. He went on to add a strip of land carrying a stream to Margate Harbour, known as the Dyke as well as adjoining swampland. Bordered by houses and the railway line, this area of some 20 acres was prone to flooding, ruling out use for housing.

In 1873 Reeve's son Arthur, married Harriett Sanger, daughter of the great Victorian showman 'Lord' George Sanger. The couple had met when Sanger's circus, flooded off its pitch in Margate, had been directed on to comparatively drier ground owned by the Alderman. Reeve, turning down Sanger's offer of recompense, accepted instead an invitation for his family to visit the circus and returned the hospitality by entertaining Sanger and family to tea.

At the same time as Arthur and Harriet were getting married, their fathers agreed to jointly develop The Hall By The Sea.

It should be said here that 'Lord' George Sanger

2. Although pictured around 1920, this interior view of The Hall By The Sea ballroom would have looked much the same throughout the Sanger era.

The early days

3. 'Lord' George Sanger transformed the frontage of The Hall By The Sea to depict paintings of his menagerie animals and other attractions as this view of 1876 shows.

was never a peer of the realm. He adopted his title because a rival, the American 'Buffalo Bill' Cody had been referred to in a Court case Sanger lost as 'The Honourable William Cody'. Sanger is said by his grandson to have exclaimed: "The Honourable William Cody! If that Yankee can be an Honourable, then I shall be a ruddy Lord!" The paint pot came out right away and 'Lord' prefixed his publicity posters and wagons.

Straight away he understood what would appeal to Margate's visitors and quickly made a success of the Hall. He took over in February 1874 and this was followed by a grand opening in June. The building was refurbished, becoming a restaurant by day and a ballroom at night, under the management of Arthur Reeve.

Music hall performers were brought down from London and a lively mood was ensured by the huge bar – open throughout the day unfettered by licensing laws.

The old railway building was eventually replaced with a purpose built structure designed by Richard Dalby-Reeve, architect brother of Arthur, and opened in July 1898. It was a long narrow single-storied building with a seating capacity of 1,400 for the music hall concerts held afternoon and evening throughout the

summer, after which the chairs were cleared to accommodate up to 3,000 for the dances ending the day's programme.

Sanger's imagination was at its best with his development of the land at the rear into a picturesque ornamental garden. The entrance, at the bottom of a slope beside the Hall, was an arched gateway in a perimeter wall made of flints and brick rubble from where paths led past shrubberies and rockeries to an imposing folly – a medieval ruined abbey – used as a bandstand with music played several times each day.

There were fishponds with fountains, a small lake fed from the Dyke, populated with waterfowl, and summerhouses offering shelter from the sun or rain. Cockatoos and macaws flew around quite freely.

The bordering embankment was decorated with plaster replicas of classical statuary painted to resemble marble – some said to be based on those in the papal Vatican City – while Sanger's less famous brother William, ran his own waxworks beside an array of swings, archery ranges, a coconut shy and a steam powered roundabout.

Furthest from the seafront was built the greatest attraction of all, an indoor menagerie with 23 cages for lions, tigers, leopards, bears,

4. The Abbey ruins in the gardens were a folly originally built during Sanger's time but still looked impressive when photographed in the 1920s. This was a publicity shot used for a number of years in park brochures.

baboons and wolves. The cages were extremely cramped and would shock modern day animal lovers. It must not be forgotten that for Victorians to see a wild animal in the flesh was both dangerous and exciting.

Away from the public gaze was a covered slaughter yard which despatched injured and worn-out horses from a wide area to be fed to the menagerie's residents.

A supply of fresh milk was guaranteed for The Hall By The Sea as cows grazed on lush marshy meadows beyond the gardens. Residents bringing jugs would also queue outside the cowshed at milking time.

Thomas Dalby Reeve died in April 1875 and Sanger purchased the freehold of the site, increasingly taking the part of prominent Margate citizen. He bought clothing and coal for the 'deserving poor' and presided at the subsequent distribution ceremonies in the Hall with the Mayor, the local vicar and others.

In April 1893, to cater for another great craze, a roller skating rink was opened at the Hall with an 8,000 square foot ivory maple floor. Daily demonstrations were given by Professor Chambers 'the skateorial king' who also provided 'instructions to ladies and gentlemen in ease and comfort and without the slightest chance of falling'.

Access to the gardens from the ballroom was through a tunnel built under the rink, one side of which was lined with ferns, the other an aquarium and aviary. This was where in 1895 the circus strong man met a woman who promised him a 'good time' in the gardens. When she didn't live up to expectations, he strangled her and left her body among the plants. Her screams were drowned by the cries of the animals and birds disturbed by a firework display at the time.

The strong man was discovered and later hanged but is immortalised in the 1860s view of The Hall By The Sea as one of the seafront bystanders – see page five. The ghost of the fated young woman is said to still haunt that part of Dreamland.

Hundreds of coloured lanterns were hung in the trees to light the gardens after dark. These contained tightly packed slow burning

The early days

5. Some of the Hall's lions who were captured for the camera around 1913.

gunpowder and had to be taken down, replenished and rehung nightly – an arduous task until the Hall became one of the first venues in Margate to have electricity.

Animals bred and trained by succeeding menagerie keepers were sent all over Europe and for years many circuses and menageries owned an animal named Margate. Some of the greatest successes were achieved by George Sadler who at times would be sharing his cottage in the grounds with up to 20 lion cubs who needed bottle feeding.

In 1899 Sadler's animal husbandry resulted in an unusual pairing of a lion cub with a lamb and, after a spell on display in the gardens, they joined Sanger's Circus where a lion was always paraded on a tableau wagon crouched at the feet of a 'Brittania'. In those days of Empire, a lion and a lamb gave an added patriotic dimension.

Another leonine protegy was Emperor, christened by King Oscar of Sweden when Sadler took the lion cub to a party on board the king's yacht at Ramsgate.

Emperor was taught to walk two tightropes stretched over the lake in the gardens. One night Emperor was startled by a firework display. He lost his balance, fell into the water, swam out and ran soaking wet to Sadler's cottage!

When Sadler married in October 1900 he and his bride Ellen cut their wedding cake in the lions' cage. A few of the guests boldly accepted the couple's invitation to join them and drink a toast with the lions beside them.

In 1905, aged nearly 80, Sanger sold his circus and the Hall's menagerie, dispersing the animals. The sale only raised £350, with Emperor the lion accounting for £125. Sold to EH Bostock's menagerie in Glasgow, the animal pined for Sadler who later made the journey north of the border.

Sanger died tragically in 1911 aged 86. He had a large house at Finchley, north London, where he accused his manservant Herbert Cooper of stealing £50. A relation, Harry Austin, sacked Cooper and appointed a replacement named Jackson. Some weeks later Cooper entered the home and attacked Jackson with a razor. Austin dashed out from a nearby room where he had been reading to Sanger. Cooper rushed at Austin and felled him with a hatchet. Sanger rose from his chair to intervene, seizing a heavy candelabrum from the mantelpiece. Cooper knocked this aside causing it to fall with force on Sanger's head. He collapsed in an inert heap. Seeing what he had done Cooper leapt out of a window and ran.

Although Sanger seemed to recover from the experience and to be none the worse during the evening, he died that night. Jackson was not seriously wounded but Austin was taken to hospital where he later recovered. Two days later Cooper's body was found on the Great Northern Railway between Highgate and Crouch End. Cooper had committed suicide.

Sanger's demise and subsequent funeral at Margate made national news. In pouring rain silent

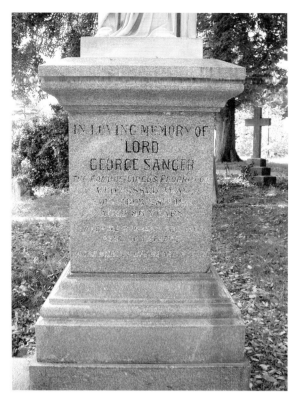

and bareheaded crowds gathered on the seafront to watch his huge polished oak coffin, emblazoned with bizarre Masonic symbols, being carried out of the Hall to take its place at the head of a procession of 50 carriages. The first three of these were almost covered by 123 floral emblems.

Blinds were drawn and businesses closed – some all day – and cabbies had black bows tied to their whips. The cortege was met at the cemetery by the Mayor and entire town council with

6. Left, 'Lord' George is remembered with a modest plaque. 7. Above, a contemporary cameo of the great showman. 8. Below, the imposing Sanger family memorials at Margate Cemetery. It is brother John whose grave is expensively topped with a Mazeppa circus horse.

9. The cover from a 1913 souvenir programme showed there was much to enjoy at The Hall By The Sea, by then under the personal direction of Mr and Mrs Arthur Reeve.

representatives from the dozen or more local organisations with which Sanger had associations. Even in death the consummate showman provided Margate with a day of diversion.

Ownership of The Hall By The Sea had passed to Arthur and Harriet Reeve who worked at raising its appeal to the better class of holiday maker otherwise attracted to Cliftonville and the newly opened Winter Gardens.

The ballroom and dance programme included regular masquerades and costume balls. There were carnival novelty nights with prize competitions in the skating rink and fetes were held in the gardens. An old fashioned, genteel atmosphere was cultivated – notices at the seafront entrance read 'Close dancing, Turkey Trot, Bunny Hug or any other Negro freakish dances are strictly forbidden in this ballroom'.

The Hall By The Sea remained open throughout the First World War, albeit at a reduced level, but by

10. The entertainment programme for a week in September 1913 at the Reeve managed Hall.

HALL-BY-THE-SEA,
MARGATE.

Great Christmas Attractions.

BOXING NIGHT.

Grand Fancy Dress Ball.

FANCY DRESS OPTIONAL.

1st and 2nd PRIZES FOR BEST DRESSED LADY & GENTLEMAN.

LARGE CHRISTMAS TREE.

Dancing from 7.30 p.m. to 12 Midnight.

Price of Admission - 2s. 6d.

NEW YEAR'S EVE.

Grand Bal Masque

WONDERFUL NEW MAPLE DANCING FLOOR,

acknowledged by experts to be one of the best in England.

From 7.30 p.m. to 12.30 a.m.

Price of Admission - 2s. 6d.

HARRINGTON'S LONDON JAZZ BAND ENGAGED AT GREAT EXPENSE.

LIGHT REFRESHMENTS SERVED.　　COMFORTABLY HEATED LOUNGE.

EXTENSION OF LICENSE.

The New Management beg to announce that the Hall will be Open Daily after Boxing Night.　Dancing from 7.30 to 10.30 p.m.　Doors open 7 p.m.　Admission 2/6.

11. Poster for what was the very first event at the Hall under the ownership of John Henry Iles at the end of 1919.

1919 the style of the business was becoming jaded. The Reeves, now in their sixties, decided it was time for a well earned retirement.

At the end of November it was announced the Hall had been sold for £40,000 to a new owner. He was 47 year old John Henry Iles who arrived in Margate one afternoon, looked around the site, wrote a cheque for the deposit during tea with the elderly couple and was on his way again – all in just two hours.

As a wealthy owner of an advertising agency, Iles had been able to indulge his passion for brass bands. He organised and sponsored festivals and edited a specialist magazine, The British Bandsman – but in 1906, while on world tour with a band, he was so impressed with the obvious profitability of American amusement parks he sold his business to a partner and launched into a new career.

During subsequent holidays in Margate, he decided The Hall By The Sea could be transformed into an American style amusement park and resolved to buy it.

12. John Henry Iles decided not to make any immediate changes to the gardens after he took over – enabling popular pony rides to continue.

He already had one of Britain's earliest Scenic Railways running at Blackpool's South Shore. He built another for the Franco-British Exhibition in London in 1908 and went on to develop complete amusement parks in cities around the world including Paris, Berlin, Barcelona and Pittsburgh, calling them after the two most famous amusement parks at New York's Coney Island, either Luna Park or Dreamland.

It was this latter name that he chose for his new venture at Margate gradually phasing the old one out by using the title 'Dreamland Hall' for a few months.

Over the next 15 years Iles was to spend more than £500,000 developing Dreamland. To superintend the project he brought to Margate, as his works manager and engineer, Edmund Mancey who had been apprenticed to Magnus Volk, and on whose experience of Volk's Railway at Brighton Iles had been able to draw when he had first entered the amusement business.

Iles' initial move was to install a new floor in the ballroom, convert the old bar into a cocktail lounge and provide professional tuition in the latest tango dances by MC and manager Alan Clare.

The ballroom was 275 feet long and 55 feet wide. It was decorated throughout with mirrors on which were painted beautifully coloured animals and birds, and lined with ornamental trusses supporting over two dozen different statues.

The roof was hung with draperies and festoons. During the 1920s, stripped of most of this ornamentation it would become Dreamland's first cinema.

The gardens stayed as they were and were used for afternoon teas and concerts by Iles' beloved brass bands. Drainage of the adjoining fields commenced at once and by March 1920 the first stage in the development of the amusement park was begun on approximately the top half of the site.

It would be another 10 years before the lower half could be used for more than firework displays and as a football pitch by Margate Football Club whose home ground it had been since September 1912.

Dreamland, Margate
(TWO MINUTES FROM THE RAILWAY STATION)

PALAIS - DE - DANSE
Dancing Every Evening
In the GLORIOUS HALL OF MIRRORS. FULL LONDON ORCHESTRA.
Fully Licensed.
ADMISSION, 1/6. Except Special Carnival Nights, for details of which see other Bills.

Sunday Concerts
Every Sunday Evening, FULL LONDON PROGRAMMES.
Many Famous Artistes Engaged.
Reserved Seats Booked in Advance at the Hall, or at Thornton Bobby's, Northdown Road, Cliftonville.

Musical Teas
The Hall is Open every Afternoon for TEAS & ICES, 2.30 to 5.30.
ADMISSION FREE.   FULL ORCHESTRA.   POPULAR PRICES.

Dreamland Park
The most Up-to-date Amusement Centre on the South Coast. Many Novel and Exciting Attractions. Delightful Tea Gardens. Magnificent Scenic Railway to be Opened shortly.
ADMISSION FREE !   ADMISSION FREE !

Zoological Gardens
Finest Collection of Wild Animals at any Seaside Resort. Completely re-organised. Lions, Lionesses, Leopards, Pumas and Bears, with a host of others.   OPEN 10 TILL DUSK.

Clifton Baths Estate
(ALL TRAMS STOP AT THE ENTRANCE)

Clifton Cinema
Largest Screen and Largest Pictures in Margate. Fine Programme of Exclusive Films
Performances Daily, 2.45, 6.30 & 8.30.   POPULAR PRICES.

Clifton Concert Hall
Indoors and Outdoors combined.   LESLIE FULLER'S FAMOUS "PED'LER'S" CONCERT PARTY.   Twice Daily, 3.15 and 8 p.m.
Special Sunday Evening Concerts.

The Cliff Tea Gardens
Magnificent Sea Views.   Ideal conditions.

Swimming Bath
The only structure of its kind in Thanet. Sea Bathing with the chill off.

Warm Baths
The only Public Baths in Margate. Fresh or Sea Water Ozone Baths; a speciality widely recommended by the Medical Profession

Sea Bathing
A large number of well appointed Bathing Machines. Attendants always present.

Ye Old English Fair
(NEAR THE PIER AND HARBOUR)
All the Fun of the Fair. Gaiety and Frolic from beginning to end.   Margate's Merriest Spot.

Dalby Square Sports Ground
Right on the Front, yet sheltered. Hard Tennis Courts specially constructed.

Clarke & Knapp, Printers, Margate.

13. An early handbill, circa late 1920, advertising the delights of Dreamland and the Clifton Baths Estate – which would become the Lido, Cliftonville.

14. *Sedate Devonshire cream teas could be enjoyed in the shadow of the Scenic Railway when the park first opened.*

A time of prosperity

A Joy Wheel, a Haunted Castle, a House of Nonsense, a Cake Walk, a Helter Skelter and numerous side shows greeted the first visitors to Dreamland on its opening day on 3 July 1920. The Dreamland Miniature Railway was completed just in time and firework displays by the firm Brock & Co were planned.

Even so there was still an air of sparseness as a result of a post war shortage of materials, limited time, money and the need for lighter constructed buildings because of the ground conditions.

The Joywheel was brought from the Clifton Baths Estate at Cliftonville and rebuilt in the park. On this contraption up to 20 people sat for a circular ride. As it got faster and faster they would start to fall off, till only one was left. These first attractions would be enhanced the following year by a Lunar Ball – Britain's first – and two other rides which had only previously been seen at London's Olympia, The Whip and The Tumble Bug.

Back then, as it would be for so long, it was the Scenic Railway which was the centrepiece. This mammoth construction of Canadian douglas fir cost more than £20,000 and, with a track length of nearly a mile, was one of the largest of its kind.

Iles had obtained the European rights on Scenic Railways building them at a number of British and Continental amusement parks before the First World War – so it was an easy decision to build another in Margate.

The Scenic Railway was an instant hit. In the 13 weeks of the remaining summer season it carried more than half a million delighted passengers. In 1921, its first full season, it carried nearly a million.

Even on the day before the official opening hundreds had packed on to its trains when it operated for charity. The takings were duly presented to the Mayor of Margate for the Cottage Hospital fund at a formal celebration lunch held in the Hall of Mirrors. This local dignitary actually received a large bag of cash – no giant sized cheques in those days!

The success of the Scenic Railway, whose profits alone were reckoned to be enough to pay the debenture-holders in the new Margate Estates holding company, encouraged the later construction of a similar but gentler ride – the

Racing Coaster. These two car trains ran on castors rather than rails and were guided on their journey by rubbing boards.

During his speech at the lunch, Iles said he believed, correctly as it turned out, that Dreamland would have an important bearing on the future prosperity of Margate. More varied entertainments than the borough yet offered would prove greatly advantageous and increase the popularity and prosperity of the resort.

A week after the opening the Isle of Thanet Gazette reported: "Visitors and residents who flocked to Dreamland Hall and Gardens have been astonished at the metamorphosis created by the army of workmen throughout the winter and spring.

"The great Scenic Railway has at once captivated the public imagination and its trains have been running in almost ceaseless succession.

"The Zoo has been brought up to date and many new animals added. An enormous kitchen has been constructed, making it possible to cater for holiday parties of 1,500, besides providing for the regular daily demand."

15. Another trainload of funseekers hold on to their hats as they whirl around the track.

16. The gardens brought a calming influence to the park in the 1920s.

Another popular attraction was the Miniature Railway. Its 15 inch gauge rails ran for 600 yards around the park, over two lattice steel bridges, under a third, across a five span wooden viaduct and a level crossing. There was also a loco shed and a station complete with coal store and signals, adjoining a new secondary entrance to the park at Eaton Road away from the seafront. Construction of this elaborate little track was led by well known miniature railway engineer Henry Greenly (later knighted) who went on to build the Romney Hythe & Dymchurch Railway with its owner Captain John Howey.

Dreamland's locomotives were Prince Edward and Billie, the latter arriving in 1928 from Rhyl. Like so many steam engines they had personalities of their own and were revered by visitors and staff for many years.

As more rides were brought to the park in successive years so the track was reduced until it was about half its original length but the attraction was given a new station complete with engine traverser to ease shunting after each round trip.

DREAMLAND PARK,
MARGATE,
Will be Opened to the Public
ON
SATURDAY, JULY 3rd.

It will provide the most fascinating up-to-date and enjoyable
AMUSEMENTS CENTRE
In the Isle of Thanet.

Its attractions include
Giant Scenic Railway
Joy Wheel
Haunted Castle
House of Nonsense
Miniature Railway
And a host of other THRILLING, EXCITING, and INTERESTING EVENTS.

SATURDAY, JULY 3rd.

17. Advertisement from the Isle of Thanet Gazette announcing Dreamland's impending opening.

18. Dreamland's Miniature Railway, designed by Henry Greenly, featured on an early 1920s postcard depicting the station in the gardens.

THE MINIATURE RAILWAY
DREAMLAND, MARGATE

A time of prosperity

19. The Caterpillar soon after arrival in 1922 showing the covers rolled only halfway.

1922 saw the introduction of The Caterpillar. Iles had bought the sole European rights for this ride the previous year, thus making it another ride always associated with Dreamland. For many years he ran Caterpillars at a number of British and continental amusement parks, each the subject of an individual operating company. Dreamland's Caterpillar would last longest until the early 1980s.

Countless thousands were whisked round an 80 feet diameter undulating track at increasing speed, suddenly plunged into darkness by a cover and startled by wailing klaxons. After a few minutes the hood would be just as suddenly folded back to coincide with a blast of compressed air blown under each rider, often raising ladies' skirts right over their heads – much to the hilarity of numerous bystanders.

20. A view of the park, probably at the end furthest from the seafront, by which time rides such as The Racing Coaster were becoming established favourites.

21. *The gardens looked particularly tranquil in the 1920s with a river running through the middle.*

The Empire Exhibition at the then all new Wembley stadium in 1924 was the source of the third of Dreamland's longest lasting rides – The River Caves, demolished in 1984. Colloquially known as The Tubs, passengers sat in huge metal bins gliding along a swift flowing waterway through a series of plaster and cement constructed caves.

These included the Ice Cave, the Smugglers' Cave and the Venetian Cave. A sedate ride, its basic wooden construction and primitive waterwheel mechanism meant it required even more maintenance than the Scenic Railway. Although aimed mainly at a family audience, many a romantic couple would take advantage of the dark seclusion it provided.

Tragedy struck the park in June 1928 when four people were killed – Dreamland's first fatalities – as a newly installed ride came apart one afternoon.

The Atlantic Flyer consisted of eight flying boats, each capable of carrying eight people, which were suspended on steel struts and were rotated in roundabout style.

A metal pin at the end of one boat's struts sheared, tilting the craft and flinging its eight occupants in all directions among the crowd 20 feet below. Three were killed instantly, one a 16 year old boy, and a fourth died on the way to hospital. The inquest revealed two had broken their necks while the others had died from skull fractures. The other occupants were seriously injured.

The Flyer's owner and operator Fritz Schmidt was among many naturally devastated by the incident and when selling on the ride a short time later, asked people to 'refrain from making unreasonable offers as my nerves are shattered'.

22. *Statues in the gardens were said to be similarly styled to those in the Vatican City.*

23. The Garden Café, largest of Dreamland's restaurants, laid up for 1,200 people in 1928.

Two aircraft hangars played an important part in Dreamland's development for several years. Measuring 200 feet long, they had originally been ordered by the US Coastguard Service during the First World War but with the end of hostilities in 1918 they had become surplus to requirements. After some negotiation they arrived in Margate in kit form for assembly.

One housed an arcade of an increasing number of stalls and sideshows while the other provided the shell of what became known as the Garden Café.

This was capable of seating up to 1,200 people – easily the largest of seven, and later eight, restaurants around the park. These were the heydays of the works and factory beanfeast outings. Dozens of charabancs, and later streamlined motor coaches, would disgorge their passengers in Dreamland's own coach park. Those arriving on specially chartered trains only had a short stroll to make before reaching their destination.

Mass catering was an important part of Dreamland's business for 30 years and it was common for parties of several hundred to sit down for lunch together. All told, the restaurants

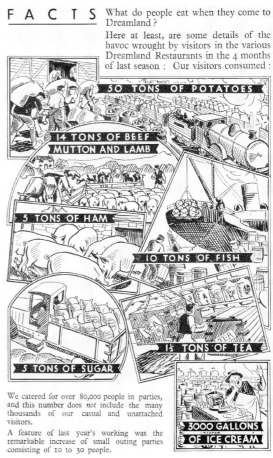

FACTS What do people eat when they come to Dreamland?

Here at least, are some details of the havoc wrought by visitors in the various Dreamland Restaurants in the 4 months of last season: Our visitors consumed :

50 TONS OF POTATOES

14 TONS OF BEEF MUTTON AND LAMB

5 TONS OF HAM

10 TONS OF FISH

1½ TONS OF TEA

5 TONS OF SUGAR

3000 GALLONS OF ICE CREAM

We catered for over 80,000 people in parties, and this number does *not* include the many thousands of our casual and unattached visitors.

A feature of last year's working was the remarkable increase of small outing parties consisting of 10 to 30 people.

24. Just some idea of how much food was eaten by beanfeasters at the height of summers in the 1920s.

25. Members of a 1923 outing pose for a group photo outside the cinema entrance. Note the entertainers sat in the centre of the front row.

could accommodate 3,500 people. In the early 1930s Dreamland's claim to be the largest caterer in the country was entirely justified with more than 130,000 customers a year. The catering manager John Forbes earned an enviable reputation as a result.

26. Right, The JazzIts band, pictured in 1922, was probably typical of those hired to provide music during lunches.

27. Lightning service was a proud boast of the well equipped and staffed kitchens.

All this feeding and watering demanded a large team to ensure everything was served on time. Accordingly, there were three well equipped kitchens, a butchery, bakery and an ice factory. Teams of chefs provided 'lightning service' the management claimed in its brochures of the day.

Hot lunches started at three shillings and sixpence a head (18p) and included soup, and a choice of roast beef and Yorkshire pudding or roast mutton with vegetables. Dessert choices were fruit tart and custard sauce or jelly.

For those paying the top six shillings each (30p) the choice widened to offer fried fillet of sole or roast lamb or chicken. In 1931, these

A time of prosperity

28. A busy day in the park shows the Winchester Rifle range, centre, and the roundabout in full use.

delights could be washed down with a bottle of white wine from four shillings and sixpence (23p) or a bottle of beer – Guinness, pale ale or milk stout – at sevenpence halfpenny each (about 4p). A bottle of quality champagne was priced at 18 shillings (90p).

Until the early fifties Dreamland made all its own ice cream which was also sold wholesale to hotels and shops, together with the wrappers and spoons. Also its own bread and cakes could be bought by the public from a small shop at the front of the bakery. The wrapped Dreamland loaf became famous and was produced for resale around the district.

29. Repeat rides on the Scenic Railway were only 6d when this view, showing the original arcade, was taken.

In 1923 it was decided to capitalise on the booming silent movie business by converting the ballroom into a 900 seat cinema. This opened on 17 May with a 13 piece orchestra providing the music and sound effects for Hall Caine's great epic of the era – The Prodigal Son. The addition a few months later of a small stage enabled variety acts such as Ken and Mac – twa draps o' Scotch – and Raglas the international juggler to also appear in what was then called the Dreamland Variety Cinema.

At the same time the old roller skating rink was transformed into a large ballroom with a Tudor style decoration and a mosaic marble floor.

The original Noterman organ, dating from the opening of the building 36 years earlier, was restored and opened in August 1929. The following April talkies were introduced.

Despite all this work on the cinema it became obvious within a few years that it could not compete with others nearby, namely the Astoria and Regal. Both had been earmarked as super cinemas to stand out from the other old fashioned establishments around the town at the time.

30. Right, front cover of a guide to Dreamland. Hundreds of thousands were given away every summer.

31. Inside Dreamland's first cinema during the silent era of the 1920s.

32. The frontage of Dreamland cinema in 1933, just before it was demolished to make way for the new complex.

Margate Estates management decided a project ambitious enough to be the last word in comfort and style was needed. An era of skyscrapers, neon lights, positive features and bold use of glass had arrived.

Distinguished architects Julian Leathart and WF Grainger were commissioned to design a new complex containing a super cinema, ballroom, restaurant, bars and lounges.

They were to be assisted by John Bird Iles, John Henry's second son, an interior designer. He was responsible for the elegant scheme of polished wood dado surrounding the auditorium with sea gods and nymphs set into the walls – a sentimental link with the statues around the walls of the old Hall By The Sea.

Work began at the end of the summer season in 1933. During the following year the Sunshine Café, with its panoramic views over Margate seafront, was completed and opened in time for the Whitsun holiday. That September work

33. An isometric drawing of part of the new building as shown in Building magazine, June 1934. It carried an extensive feature on the work in hand.

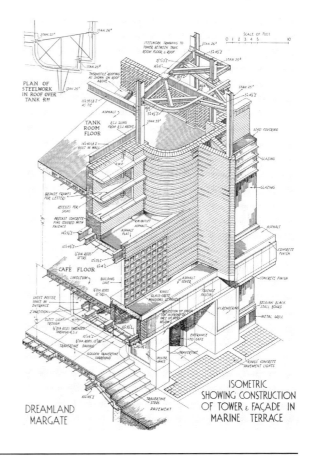

ISOMETRIC
SHOWING CONSTRUCTION
OF TOWER & FAÇADE IN
MARINE TERRACE

DREAMLAND
MARGATE

Dreamland Remembered   **23**

A time of prosperity

began on the massive auditorium of the cinema and the adjoining maple floored ballroom.

Standing at 80 feet tall, this art deco inspired creation would be the tallest building along Margate seafront for the next 30 years – its fin like outline proving the ideal beacon to Dreamland. Plans and drawings soon appeared in architectural journals thus influencing the shape of many more similar structures for years afterwards.

The opening night souvenir programme of March 1935 notes the building was fully air-conditioned by a complex system of fans

Facing page, 34. Top, an artist's impression of how the new cinema would look at night from the seafront and 35. Inside the new Sunshine Café, as photographed by Building magazine in 1934.

This page, 36. Builders hadn't quite finished work when this view of the building was taken. Note the lines of the Isle of Thanet Electric Tramway in the road surface.

A time of prosperity

and reveals that 20 miles of heavy duty electrical cable were installed along with two acres of carpet and linoleum. The building also used 1.5 million bricks, 700 tons of cement and four acres of plaster as well as one and a half acres of glass.

The ground work had proved difficult to handle and eventually consisted of 10 feet of top soil on a silt base over sand and loose chalk. Reinforced concrete piles had to be driven down to around 25 feet.

Inside, the cinema could take 2,200 people in comfy tip up seats in its stalls and balcony – all to watch one very large screen. Local MP Capt Harold Balfour performed the official opening ceremony and the invited dignitaries were able to celebrate with a buffet of oysters and champagne. They watched Greta Garbo star in her latest movie, The Painted Veil, along with the Laurel and Hardy comedy, Them Thar Hills, as well as a British Movietone newsreel. Worryingly, that newsreel included items such as Germany asserting its right to re-arm. Other items about the French liner Normandie and London's police

horses getting ready for that year's Royal Silver Jubilee were more in keeping with the occasion.

Outside, a smartly dressed commissionaire greeted patrons as they arrived. Ten usherettes saw people to their seats. Stalls were priced at 6d (2.5p), 9d (4p), one shilling (5p) and one and six (7.5p). For the more affluent, balcony seats were priced at one and six and two shillings (10p). Pink carpets lined the foyer floors with blue settees and easy chairs dotted around to bring a relaxing, stylish ambience. Glass and pottery ashtrays were provided – but all of these had disappeared within a week.

In those days, no cinema was complete without its organ and organist which would rise majestically through the floor on a lift before every performance. Lewis Gerard was maestro of the many keyboards of Dreamland's Compton which had cost £4,850 to install. Somewhat inevitably the song Meet Me Tonight in Dreamland quickly became his signature tune. Within a few months Lewis was as much a star there as the Hollywood screen actors who followed after his performances.

Facing page, 37. Top, the impressive interior of Dreamland cinema in 1935. This photo was still being used to promote the place in the late 1960s and, 38. The art deco foyer. The ticket booth is now a listed structure.

39. Organist Lewis Gerard, pictured after his return in 1947, became an instant star of the cinema.

Speaking of those days during the 1970s he recalled: "I had a horror of two things – talking to the audience and raising the organ lift for my performances. To my mind, they were never very reliable. At the final rehearsal on the night before the opening ceremony, I had concluded my solo and turned around to say something to Eric Iles when 'wham' – down the organ went about 14 feet – and fast. Fortunately no one was hurt and there was no damage to the organ. Eric Iles was unbelievable, he never flapped and just peered over the top of the orchestra rail and asked: 'Are you in distress?' You know, I couldn't even answer him."

The organ typifies the art deco style of those years, housed in a jelly mould collection of illuminated coloured glass panels. The console has four manual keyboards, 215 stops, a waterfall effect in the illuminated panels and, a revelation for the mid thirties, sounds to control a solo cello and percussion effects such as glockenspiel, xylophone, drums and cymbals – all of these housed in five rooms above the stage. The organ could also control a grand piano standing on the stage. A visual device called the Brenograph created a kaleidoscope of coloured designs on the screen.

The Compton is still in working order today thanks to the hard work and dedication of the Margate Theatre Organ Club which has owned and restored it over a number of years.

Harold Finch was appointed manager of the new complex after the death of popular top-hatted predecessor Jack Binns in 1934. Though before he died he had seen the plans, Jack did not live to see their completion. Such was his personal esteem that his funeral cortege passed as close as possible to Dreamland, crossing on the wrong side of Marine Terrace to approach within a few feet of his beloved cinema which, naturally, was closed for the afternoon.

40. Top, manager Jack Binns, who died before he could see the new cinema.

41. Examples of show cards advertising the month's programme at the cinema. These date from July, August and September 1935 and would have been familiar sights in local hotels and guest houses.

A time of prosperity

42. Wreckage of the 1930 fire which claimed a number of rides, sideshows and a roundabout.

The park had seen a fair amount of restructuring as the 1930s arrived – mainly out of necessity owing to a damaging fire. A combination of wooden buildings erected throughout the 1920s and widespread cigarette smoking was a recipe for disaster. In September 1930, the central arcade – one of the old aircraft hangars – caught fire completely destroying sideshows housed therein. Several nearby rides such as the Rapids and Over The Falls also disappeared in the inferno. More than £20,000 worth of damage was caused in little over an hour.

The Isle of Thanet Gazette reported the blaze had started soon after park closing time at 11pm and the fire brigade had arrived within a couple of minutes. Flames shot up to 120 feet high and could be seen for miles around, drawing an estimated crowd of 5,000 to watch the drama unfold.

There were no serious injuries and a pet greyhound named Sweet Dolly, chained up in an office by the Haunted House, was released by police.

The newspaper robustly refuted national media claims that firemen ran short of water and had to pump sea water on to the flames instead. The Eaton Road hydrant had proved sufficient, said the Gazette, and it was business as normal the following day with the remaining attractions in operation.

Arising from the ashes the following year was a brand new concrete structured arcade, much larger and better than before. Close by a Motor Boats ride was introduced. The chance to replace other wooden structures in the vicinity was also taken and along with newly laid out gardens and flower beds the park took on a more unified and tidier appearance.

Fire struck again early one morning in August 1937 destroying staff rooms and workshops. Fifty

43. The arcade and nearby rides were well alight when this dramatic scene was captured of the 1930 blaze.

44. The new arcade was ready for the 1931 season and looks imposing with the Motor Boats ride in the foreground.

waitresses lost their uniforms and a season's tips, leaving a few almost penniless. The blaze spread to a paint store, gutted a glass-cutting room, the plumber's department, bill posting and publicity rooms as well as wrecking a store containing weekly magazines belonging to Amalgamated Press.

Strong winds fanned the flames towards the firework store, setting off some of the smaller varieties. Larger set pieces were untouched, still enabling that week's display to go ahead.

45. The Motor Boats ride itself, fun to navigate around its winding course and fun to watch from the footbridge over.

A time of prosperity

46. All change at the miniature railway in the 1930s.

47. Right, the train runs through the gardens in 1934.

The successful career of John Henry Iles came to an abrupt end in February 1938. He had invested heavily in a film production company making movie shorts, some starring comedian Leslie Fuller who had graduated to film stardom after appearing with his concert party at Cliftonville. Iles had put in £250,000 rebuilding the Rock Studios at Elstree. The venture failed and he was declared bankrupt owing £351,000.

48. Let's hope the engine's boiler wasn't too hot when these young ladies clambered aboard in 1938.

49. Dreamland's founder John Henry Iles, left, with the Duke of Kent at Belle Vue, Manchester, in 1932.

50. *A view of the park taken in the immediate years prior to World War Two.*

51. *Flexing for fun in the gardens, circa 1938.*

Disqualified from his directorships he had to exchange his mansion, Gap House, at Dumpton for a bungalow in Herschell Road, Birchington. He began writing again for the British Bandsman and was awarded the OBE in 1944 for his services to brass music. He died in 1951.

His interests were taken over by son Eric and son-in-law Howard Goldby. Within a year Eric was in sole charge. Eric was more cautious than his father and halted further development of Dreamland while making stringent economies. Lewis Gerard, who earned a high salary befitting his status, volunteered to leave as he could – and did – easily find another post. He played himself out in March 1938 and would not return for another nine years.

Rumours began to spread about the future of Dreamland but they were unfounded and the business was still intact at the outbreak of war in September 1939.

The park closed immediately but the ballroom and the cinema kept going although Eric Iles had

52. A horse and jockey canter along the beach to race to Dreamland – one of many promotional gimmicks to keep the customers coming.

53. Kiddies Day in September 1934 saw a massive Guy Fawkes and bonfire built as centrepiece of a special fireworks display. Children would be given paper fancy dress costumes and free rides.

Happiness like this means "Dreamland" for you!

MARGATE'S WONDER AMUSEMENT PARK

FIREWORKS EVERY THURSDAY
and
HARRY ROY'S LYRICALS in THE GREAT BALLROOM

put the company into voluntary liquidation, unable to see any prospect of it trading profitably until hostilities came to an end.

In June 1940 the entire site was requisitioned by the Government for a different kind of welcome to Margate. This was the Dunkerque evacuation which saw thousands of troops pour into towns along the East Kent coast.

The restaurants became first aid centres and a procession of stretchers and a seemingly endless stream of walking wounded kept volunteers busy offering what treatment they could. They also wrote hundreds of post cards with the jubilant message 'Safe in England' which were posted to homes all over the country.

Meanwhile the ballroom became a large dormitory. Beds and bedding were brought in and settees, originally used for resting weary dancers now comforted those who had, only hours before, limped off the Dunkerque sand dunes.

54. Smiles all round on this handbill from 1936.

55. Park view showing the Caterpillar, left, Motor Boats, sideshows and Scenic Railway where a peak capped ride attendant is collecting fares.

56. A line of sandwich board men prepare to walk their beats advertising Dare Devil Peggy, a one legged high diver, in 1930. Peggy would dive 60 feet into a small tank of water.

A wrinkled old French woman who had trudged miles to reach a boat still clutched her pet dog. Although weary she kept up her spirits frequently shouting 'Vive La France' but her real grief came when she was told her dog had to be taken away and put in quarantine. She wept bitterly.

In happier mood were two Belgian girls who had made their way to Dunkerque and, anxious to reach England, had somehow acquired two soldiers uniforms. One observer noted Dreamland seemed like a fairyland to them. The Garden Café became an interrogation centre for it was always possible that a fifth columnist had been planted among the hundreds of soldiers and civilians being landed in the town.

Later in the war, the ballroom was taken over by the Ministry of Supply to make camouflage material.

The coach and car parks were very useful for parking vehicles and storage space.

57. The Trainair flight simulators were popular in 1937.

58. In 1937 the Royal Coronation Midgets spent the season at Dreamland and were soon at work building their summer quarters. The public paid to see them go about their daily chores and watch their acrobatic displays.

59. Secretaries organising beanfeast outings received copies of this letter in Spring 1940 telling them Dreamland was still very much open for business. The Dunkerque evacuation and war requisition soon put a stop to fun in the park.

Dreamland picked up its fair share of scars during the war, fire bombs fell several times near the park boundaries and a long range shell blew away part of the cinema wall. The other local cinemas, the Astoria and Regal, were not so fortunate, both being completely destroyed in different air raids.

Meanwhile, Len Mancey, son of John Henry Iles' right hand man Edmund Mancey, became caretaker manager of Dreamland during these darkened years. He formed his own band to hold dances in the Garden Café for the Red Cross prisoner of war fund. These events were well attended by soldiers billeted in the town and returning residents – by the time the war was over the dances had raised £8,000.

A time of prosperity

60. It's ladies only for this publicity shot of the Brooklands Racers in 1949 as Dreamland got into its stride after WW2.

Post war revival

This was the era of demob suits and gratuities, with fun starved families flocking to the seaside for the first time in years to recover from the pressures of war and escape, albeit briefly, from a world still bogged down by rationing. In short, millions were determined to have some fun.

One of the first jobs that had to be done to get Dreamland in shape once more was to demolish two one million gallon water tanks planted in the car park by the Army. A six year growth of grass and weeds also had to be removed.

Apart from physical obstructions there was a large lack of maintenance to make up. On top of that a variety of licences, such as those for building materials and timber, had to be obtained, often with considerable difficulty.

The park reopened in June 1946 with the cinema and ballroom following a month later. Even the few hastily prepared stalls and rides were an unqualified success -- a sign of great prosperity to follow.

61. The Motor Boats were quick to regain their popularity after 1945.

62. Crowds throng the sideshows and rides in 1950, taking the chance to get away from austerity for a few hours.

63. Eric Iles, who put Dreamland back on its feet after WW2 and continued at the helm until late 1970.

Eric Iles resumed his managerial mantle of Margate Estates, Dreamland's holding company. He never liked the idea of being considered a showman and was at pains to point out he was in fact an administrator. His strength of purpose and strong will enabled him to start Dreamland all over again and consolidate the business.

Showman or not, Eric was keenly perceptive about entertainment. His interest in finding new rides was unending. When trying out a ride on business trips to parks abroad, he would pass his hat and briefcase to wife Doris, carefully time it, note how long it took to load, unload and how many customers boarded. He would take a camera to picture lighting effects or novelties which might be brought to Dreamland.

The park got back on its feet again with help from holiday camp king Billy Butlin who invested £160,000 and was company Chairman between 1947 and 1954. The immediate post war years were a boom time, highlighted by the 1947 annual report revealing the company had made a profit of £104,000 and declaring a dividend of 17 per cent.

Post war revival

64. Coach parties were big business and there were at least 50 vehicles here on this summer's day in the late 1940s.

Butlin's wide contacts proved very useful in finding new attractions for production of fairground equipment which – like everything else – was in short supply. One ride he secured for the park, though not new, was a treasured Galloping Horses roundabout. When it arrived in Margate in 1946, this 19th century antiquity came complete with a French organ to supply the music. This later deteriorated and replacement parts could no longer be obtained so it was converted to electricity.

65. The Dreamland staff assemble for a group photo in front of the cinema entrance in 1946.

66. The Whirlwind ride in 1954. People still looked formally dressed for a day by the sea.

The post war public revelled in sideshows such as Tip The Lady Out of Bed in which, as the name suggests, punters were invited to cast a suitably scantily clad girl into a bath of water when a ball scored a direct hit on a tilt lever. Another woman was encased in ice while elsewhere dark skinned men played voodoo drums.

Dwarves had returned to Dreamland and had set up quarters in the number five hall near the park entrance. Often these people of restricted height would build their own home for the summer season and go about their daily chores as the paying public watched.

Thursday night was fireworks night. Displays once again became a summer attraction. They appealed to adults, who had seen nothing like them since pre-war days, as well as children who had never seen fireworks. Large crowds gathered every week to see the dazzling displays of Brock fireworks. Although these extravaganzas lasted 20 minutes, it took Dreamland's staff three days to set them up.

67. Fun on the helter skelter, as much a fairground favourite then as it is today.

A major setback to this renewed popularity came in August 1949 when the Scenic Railway caught fire, destroying at least half the structure.

The alarm was raised by 21 year old Yvonne Longhi, of nearby Marine Terrace, who woke up to see flames underneath the ride. As she was phoning the fire brigade, so the flames shot up to 50 feet. The brigade sent all nearby machines in Thanet and were joined by more from RAF Manston. The firemen had to break through locked main gates and quickly drained the boating pool before controlling the blaze.

With gas cylinders exploding and the flames working their way towards the zoo, a vet stood by ready to shoot the animals – a lioness, a bear, baboons and a baby monkey among them. Happily, he wasn't needed as the fire was contained in time.

Owing to ongoing post-war restrictions on building materials, finding enough wood to rebuild the Scenic Railway was likely to take some years to complete, the management concluded.

The answer though came in a most unlikely fashion. Eric Iles and chief engineer Jack Lynch were flying back from Denmark after viewing potential new rides when somebody noticed below the sorry war damaged remains of Lowestoft Pier. The timber was just what was needed for the Scenic Railway and enquiries about buying the wood were made almost immediately after the plane touched down. It transpired that a Portsmouth firm had bought it but agreed to sell, with official blessing, some

68. Standing up in the Scenic Railway cars has always been forbidden – but there's always one who tries.

30,000 cubic feet – or 180 standards – of Lowestoft Pier. The timber eventually arrived in Margate ready to rebuild the famous railway but one not so small job which had to be undertaken first was removal of hundreds of 10 inch nails buried deep in the wood. For years these had held the old pier together against the ravages of the North Sea.

Incidentally, the rides viewed in Denmark's national aquarium were never followed up as there were insurmountable difficulties in constantly pumping the water involved. The trip had been worthwhile as the Scenic Railway was readied in time for the 1950 season.

Dreamland park long had story value for the local and national newspapers. Even a power failure in the fifties somehow became more agreeable the next day when readers learned the River Caves had provided a useful side effect.

'A dream came true last night for couples in love... they were in Dreamland's Tunnel of Love and there was a power failure', announced a Sunday paper.

It went on to say the courting couples were isolated 'for 10 whole minutes', adding that

69. A fifties view of the Scenic Railway. Note the large greenhouses in the void space.

70. *Sleeping Beauty's castle was one of the Magic Garden's highlights when opened in 1951.*

71. *No garden was complete without its gnomes. Dreamland had an entire colony – and saucer eyed trees too.*

72. A fairytale character riding a magic swan added to the garden's glory.

stallholders had to wade through the water to push them into the open. It doesn't say what sort of reception they got!

As wartime restrictions began to ease many of Britain's bigger resorts, including rival Ramsgate, began to install elaborate sea front illuminations. In spite of pleas from the town's hotels and businesses, Margate Council would not do so.

Eric Iles decided to capitalise on this deficiency by installing £10,000 worth of decorative lighting and illuminated figures in the ornamental gardens, still attractive with the old Sanger statues and ruins, and call it The Magic Garden.

In only two months Jack Lynch and his corps of electricians and workmen produced and erected scores of enchanting and ingenious displays based on nursery rhymes, classical mythology, the circus and the jungle. There were electric snowdrops and daffodils and an Orange Grove with specially

blown lamps shaped like the fruit.

The opening of the Magic Garden in 1950 caused a sensation – in the first six evenings 15,000 people queued to view it. With the additions in 1951 of a Swiss Beer Garden and a mechanical Oompah band playing from a Tyrolean bandstand, it was one of Dreamland's most charming aspects. Not only did the half life size figures play instruments, but their heads nodded, feet tapped and eyes rolled in time to recorded music.

One of the garden's most delightful features, a detailed miniature Tudor village, was transferred in 1953 to become an attraction in its own right on Ramsgate's West Cliff. The Model Village celebrated its 50th anniversary in June 2003. Sadly, little more than a month later owner Ken Wake announced closure in September owing to vandalism and falling visitor numbers.

73. A detailed Tudor village was a centrepiece until transferred to help create the Ramsgate Model Village.

If Dreamland's fire in 1949 had been a setback, worse was to follow. One night in August 1950 holidaymakers thronged the streets, some in their nightwear, as a huge blaze destroyed the large arcade. Within minutes flames were shooting 100 feet high and the sound of small explosions rent the air. These were asbestos roof panels disintegrating in the heat. Houses in two nearby roads were evacuated by firemen who had been despatched from all over East Kent to quench the flames. It was reckoned by the end that £75,000 worth of damage had been done – all at the peak of one of Dreamland's most prosperous seasons.

Loyal staff, some returning off duty, did all they could to help but about 20 stalls were gutted and others severely damaged. A local paper report noted that in the centre of the arcade a soft drink stall remained completely untouched by the fire.

74. This photo of the Octopus Ride, centre, was taken just days before the arcade, top, burnt down in 1950.

75. Some of the tangled remains of the arcade after the great fire of 1950.

Post war revival

76. *Steam loco Billie simmers at the beginning of another day on the miniature railway in 1949.*

77. *Billie again in 1949.*

78. *Slightly obscured by a lampost, Prince Edward, nearest camera, joins Billie.*

79. An aerial view of the park captured in the mid 1950s clearly shows the 330 feet long replica of the Queen Mary. The Garden Café is to the left of the coach park and the gardens are on the right of the Scenic Railway.

The arcade had of course been built 20 years before to replace one of the former hangars that JH Iles had built for amusements which had also been lost to fire.

In 1951 a detachment of staff from Dreamland helped build the Festival of Britain's Fun Fair at Battersea Park in London. While visiting them to follow progress, Eric Iles was introduced to

80. For younger ones wanting a more sedate ride, the Peter Pan Railway provided endless enjoyment.

81. Teddy Boys were making their presence known – and sometimes felt – in the park by 1954.

Rosskilly Grundy, a designer working on another project there, and asked him to prepare a scheme for a replacement of the arcade.

Set at one end of the coach park the new structure had to have an interesting outline. It would be solid on its seaward side while housing a line of stalls on the side facing into the park. Grundy's inspired solution was a 330 feet long replica of the Cunard liner Queen Mary and despite suffering fire itself in September 1963, it dominated the amusement park for 26 years. The original refusal of Margate Council to give it permanent planning permission influenced its somewhat flimsy construction which meant that by 1977 it had deteriorated beyond repair and was demolished.

Small round cabins 15 feet deep by 25 feet in diameter were built into two of the Queen Mary's funnels. One was like a small broadcasting studio from where operator Stan Sawyer would give commentaries over the public address system for the weekly firework displays and it was his playing of the record When Day is Done that signalled the nightly closure of the park.

The other was a look out from where supervisors could keep an eye on the park and the staff. One of their tasks was called spotting. Aided by a blackboard and a pair of binoculars they would attempt to record the number of customers boarding a particular ride over a given period, later to be reconciled (or otherwise) with the cashier's records, in an effort to deter, if not detect, any dishonest practices!

82. How Dreamland celebrated the Queen's Coronation in 1953. Was the massed thanksgiving service in the coach park a success?

CORONATION CELEBRATIONS
AT
DREAMLAND
THREE GLORIOUS DAYS

SATURDAY, 30th MAY

BALLROOM · · · 7.30 p.m.—11.45 p.m. · Admn. 4/-
GREAT FESTIVE GALA
FUN, GAMES, HATS, BALLOONS & PRIZES — ALAN GREEN & HIS BAND

AMUSEMENT PARK · At Dusk. Admission to Park 1/-, Children 6d.
MAGNIFICENT DISPLAY OF BROCKS'
REGAL FIREWORKS
ALSO
PATRIOTIC SING-SONG ON ARENA GRANDSTAND--Seats 6d.

MONDAY, 1st JUNE

CINEMA
Mon., Tues., & Wed.	Thurs., Fri., & Sat.
RICHARD WIDMARK in **DESTINATION GOBI** (U) and	Robert Mitchum & Susan Hayward in **THE LUSTY MEN** (U) and
Susan Hayward & Charlton Heston in **THE PRESIDENT'S LADY** (A)	**KON-TIKI** (U)

BALLROOM · · · 7.30—11 p.m. · Admission 3/6
A CELEBRATION REVEL
SPECIAL JOLLITY NIGHT, HATS AND BALLOONS WITH ALAN GREEN

AMUSEMENT PARK · CAR PARK ARENA, 6.45 p.m.
ADMISSION TO PARK FREE
A GREAT PATRIOTIC DEMONSTRATION AND DISPLAY
FESTIVAL OF SERVICE
MARGATE TOWNSPEOPLE OFFER THEIR TRIBUTE TO THE COUNTRY
DISPLAYS AND DEMONSTRATIONS by Civil Defence, W.V.S., Sea Cadets, 438 Sqd. A.T.C., Women's Junior Air Corps 1580 (Thanet) Unit, St. John Ambulance, (Westgate and Birchington), Council of Ex-Servicemen, School Children from St. Gregory's and Draper's Mills Schools
ALSO **GRAND PARADE OF LOYALTY** *including*
The Old Contemptibles Association, British Legion, Royal Naval Association, Association of Jewish Ex-Servicemen and Women, Royal Artillery Association, Past and Present Bells, R.A.F. Association, Royal National Life Boat Institution, Margate Ambulance Corps, Margate Girl Guides, Margate Sea Rangers, British Red Cross Society (Thanet Branch), and the Association of WRENS.
Admission to Arena (6,000 Seats) : Centre Block 1/6, Child 9d.; Other Seats 1/-, Child 6d. ; Standing 9d., Child 6d. · · No charge to view C.D. Display

TUES. CORONATION DAY 2nd JUNE

SUNSHINE CAFE · · · 10 a.m.—5 p.m. (Continuous)
LARGE SCREEN TELEVISION
ALSO A BATTERY OF STANDARD SIZE T.V. SETS
SO ALL MAY SEE CEREMONY AND PROCESSION
LICENSED AND OTHER REFRESHMENTS AT POPULAR PRICES
NO CHARGE TO VIEW · · · REFRESHMENT TICKETS 6d.

AMUSEMENT PARK · · · ADMISSION FREE
GREAT OUTDOOR CARNIVAL
FREE RIDES GIVEN TO ALL IN HOME-MADE FANCY DRESS & ORIGINAL "GET-UP"
1,000's OF FREE RIDES - TREASURE HUNT CARNIVAL HATS GIVEN FREE
ROASTING THE OX WHOLE
From 2 p.m.—SIGHT OF A LIFETIME—DISTRIBUTION OF MEAT. CARVING CEREMONY, FIRST CUT BY HIS WORSHIP THE MAYOR
(Alderman H. V. WARD, J.P.)
ALSO GIANT BONFIRE

BALLROOM · · · 7.30 p.m.—1 a.m. · Admission 4/-
THE CORONATION BALL
SUNSHINE & SMILES CABARET
ROASTED OX—Meat Undistributed in Park GIVEN AWAY FREE
Hats, Balloons, Prizes & Alan Green's Band. · A Super Fun Night

SUNDAY, 7th JUNE

COACH PARK ARENA · · · 10.45 a.m. · Admission Free
MASSED THANKSGIVING SERVICE
(Interdenominational)
Organised by the Vicar of Margate. (The Rev. Sydney A. Odom)

VM/33511/F.P.C.

83. Judging by their skilful technique and smart skating boots, the two girls on the left were regular visitors to the roller rink in 1954. Compare them with the others who are less steady on their feet!

Park visitors during this time may have heard words used which were either unintelligible or gave them an entirely wrong meaning.

'I've got the swag' for instance didn't mean the person had just received proceeds from a robbery; it was merely fairground vernacular for giveaway prizes. 'Gazump' was used in fairgrounds long before it referred to house buying. Showmen used the term to describe an activity for which a lot was being charged and little in value being returned.

Roller skating enjoyed a resurgence after 1945, with competitions and gala nights for speed skating and roller dance skating. Rink hockey matches saw teams like the Dreamlandiers or Ramsgate Redwings competing against visiting teams from as far as Dartford, Brixton, Cricklewood, Southend – even Paris.

84. Winners of a fancy dress competition on the indoor rink parade in the 1950s.

85. Rumbustious goings on were the hallmark of Old Time Music Hall in the Sunshine Room.

In 1955 the Sunshine Café closed as a restaurant to become the Sunshine Theatre and the summer home of the Dreamland Old Time Music Hall presented by entertainer Alan Gale. The café's stylish decorations, including a distinctive mural by Walpole Champneys, were replaced by opulent Edwardian effects.

The audience, seated at tables in the authentic manner, were entertained to a rumbustious show – at h'enormous h'expense of course – presided by the loquatious chairman, originally Mr Thanet Friendly, in reality Dreamland's promotions manager Bill Bennett. He was succeeded by the portly and bewhiskered Ted Gatty a year or two later who in 1960 took the show over and ran it for a further eight seasons. This all started a new attraction for families who wanted to spend a merry evening with hard and soft drinks within reach and was a hint of the club style show which would change national entertainment tastes.

86. A sketch set in the parlour of the Sea View Boarding House, 1895, was all part of the Old Time fare.

87. Although Beanfeast outings were fading away in the late fifties, this one in 1957 filled the Garden Café.

The original bakery had become a dining hall, until the need for large scale catering facilities ceased with the rapid decline and disappearance in the fifties of the traditional beanfeasts. Wider car ownership and arrival of the five day working week put an end to these huge outings.

One Dreamland custom which disappeared around this time was Mother's Day. For years this was a Monday when merry parties of East End women invaded Dreamland and brought the cockney spirit to the park. Typical of these jovial jaunts was the woman – predictably there was a different one each week – who wore bloomers emblazoned with the Union Jack and cheerfully bent down to display them to passers by. Accompanied, of course, by hearty guffaws of laughter from her friends.

The old bakery then housed a number of sideshows, some presented by Alan Gale, including more or less the final appearances of Lester's Midgets – a troupe of Liliputian performers whose appearances in variety, at

88. The mind boggles at the apparent absence of safety rails as the crowd gathers to watch a motorbike stuntman go through his paces outside the Wall of Death.

89. The mini coach, based on a Leyland Tiger, was meant to ferry children between the coach and amusement parks but in 1959 these local glamour girls were given special dispensation. The mini coach was among 63 built in Brighton between 1935 and 1959 by showman Ernest Johnstone. Seventeen are thought to survive.

Battersea Fun Fair, and even in department stores, he arranged for several years in conjunction with the widow of the troupe's founder, Burton Lester.

Succeeding shows included Miranda – Margate's Modern Mermaid – actually four girls who took turns to lay submerged in a tank of water, breathing through a carefully concealed air tube; Katrina, a clairvoyant, and The Madcap Family – mechanical figures from France whose progress on a cycling holiday was shown in a series of amusing dioramas. Cars used in the Great Train Robbery were later on display together with a representation of the stolen cash.

Built underneath the Scenic Railway were two unusual attractions. There was the Canonbury Near-Beer Bar – an authentic bar in every respect except it only sold non alcoholic drinks, and which tended to attract those who wanted to

90. and 91. Road rage on the Brooklands Racers – surely not! Look closely at the two 1954 images for the two girls having a finger pointed at them for some minor misdemeanour.

92. The rock and roll house made its Dreamland debut in 1958.

93. A ballroom poster of 1957 promised entertainment six nights a week.

continue drinking after the real beer bars closed before laying out in the gardens to sleep it off.

Next to it was what came to be known as The Scenic Theatre. In it, to the accompaniment of frequent roars from the Scenic Railway trains passing overhead, a succession of bizarre shows was presented. They ranged from the semi-static Dracula's Daughter, Headless Lady and Living Half Lady, made and owned by one time magician and fire eater Jon Gresham, to short performances by well known illusionists like Al Davis and his wife with their mentalists' act, The Amazing Margoes, in 1955, and showman illusionist Knox-Crichton whose wife was The Floating Lady.

In 1960 the cinema's crop of Biblical epics in the late fifties no doubt inspired the real life impersonation of Sampson, a strongman, with Delilah, in 1958. Laurie Stagg, retiring from that great speciality act of the variety era, The Australian Air Aces, showed two illusions in the mid sixties, The Amazing Ray and Petra which

94. Dreamland's opulent ballroom was still drawing fair sized gatherings in the fifties.

was a living, talking, smiling disembodied head – both the work of Robert Harbin.

Built at one end of the Scenic Railway was Zooland, which contained a Monkey Jungle with a large cage filled with more than 40 monkeys scampering over the heads of the public passing through a mesh tunnel. This faced a horseshoe shaped range of conventional cages accommodating lions, bears, foxes, squirrels, pheasants, parrots and owls. A sudden shower of rain would attract a rush of customers to the show. When this happened Arthur Bean who ran Zooland would exhort passers by to "Come inside and see the animals under cover...see the monkeys in the dry."

95, 96. and 97. Three 1950s posters persuading outing parties to come to Margate.

98. Inside the Polynesian themed Bali Hai bar which opened on the seafront in the mid 1960s.

Anyone who complained the zoo was open to the sky was reproved with the information the cages were roofed – no one had suggested the public would not get wet! Nearby, 'Professor' Tomlin presented his flea circus. It is said his actors were sent to Margate by post from a laboratory. On one occasion, the container was damaged en route and once opened in the Dreamland offices the fleas quickly hopped out and disappeared. During the next few days everyone working there was bitten at least once! In the 1960s two responses were made in attempts to meet changing tastes in leisure pursuits. Bingo opened in the Sunshine Theatre

99. A go kart track came to the park in the early 1960s – and lads were used in the promotional photos.

Post war revival

100. A rare, but not very picturesque, photo inside the River Caves – or tubs – ride.

in November 1963 with a promise of joining in the National Lucky Scoop, a weekly accumulator and a break the bank Snowball.

Considered a passing fad which would merely generate some additional revenue in the off season, it grew so much that it became increasingly difficult to justify suspension each summer for the Old Time Music Hall, which it eventually replaced in 1969.

In the ballroom, resident dance bands gave

101. The Satellite Ride was popular for much of the 1960s.

way to single night performers. This policy of occasional engagements in the 1950s of such bands and groups as those of Ted Heath, Eric Delaney, John Barry and Ray Ellington became so popular it paved the way to appearances by all the best known bands of the time.

The last of the resident dance bands, Tommy Martin's, played out on 8 September 1962. Several hundred successful weekend appearances by Gerry and the Pacemakers, Freddie and the Dreamers, Brian Poole, Mike Berry, Carl Denver, The Springfields and The Shadows followed. The Beatles did not appear, but the Rolling Stones did – on 15 August 1963. Remarkably, Mick Jagger and Co weren't top of the bill but were supporting the Barron Knights.

The early and mid 1960s saw greater social changes and these started to have an effect on the Dreamland empire. Mods and rockers regularly converged on Margate at weekends often in violent drink fuelled clashes in the park, the seafront or on the nearby beach.

Holidays by the British seaside fell from favour as large numbers of people opted for the now widely available – and comparatively cheaper – package holidays.

102. The Sky Wheels dated from 1953.

103. This 1960s night scene shows the Sky Wheels and the Jets in the foreground. On the left a children's ride stands empty. Youngsters would have been safely in bed.

104. Outdated motorboats were replaced by the Whirl-a-boats where four or more people could easily argue over where their circular craft could be steered.

For many years after the war Dreamland cinema, like all others, competed with television to hold audiences. Despite bigger screens and more colour movies it was a losing battle.

However, no change was to be as far reaching as the sale of Margate Estates in July 1968 to Phonographic Equipment Ltd – later to become Associated Leisure Ltd – which bid £1,400,000 against two other companies who, like it, were also in the fast growing amusement machine business.

Nevertheless, no changes were immediately apparent other than a proliferation of amusement machine arcades.

Iles family control continued, for the time being at any rate, with Eric Iles remaining as Chairman, and son John becoming Managing Director.

105. Another sixties night scene. This time alongside the Scenic Railway. Note the statuary still in situ on the left hand side.

106. *The Dreamland cinema building long provided a backdrop to a packed Margate beach.*

Safari parks were becoming increasingly popular and it was decided to create one at Dreamland, for £30,000, in the ornamental gardens, where the Magic Garden, no longer a novelty, had long since closed. Kent and England cricketer, Colin Cowdrey, who performed the opening ceremony in June 1969, was able to observe history repeating itself – the site was Sanger's original pleasure garden and animal collection.

At the same time a link with the past was

107. *A general view of the Whirl-a-boats ride in 1970. The boats' unreliability won few friends among the operators.*

108. It wasn't just wild animals who could be encountered in the safari park in 1970. These young ladies were hired to show visitors around. Definitely a marked contrast from the traditional zoo keeper's style.

broken with the closure of the open air Rollerink. When the ballroom replaced Sanger's original rink, roller skating had carried on during the winter only in the Garden Café but its popularity faded in the 1930s.

John Iles left Dreamland in 1970 to become General Manager of Battersea Fun Fair. At the end of this year Eric Iles retired, to die just over 12 months later. Half a century of Iles family involvement was at an end.

109. A rare view of the frontage of the Racing Coaster, probably dating from the mid to late 1960s.

110. The racers finally got some new cars to drive. They look like scaled down versions of the Austin Cambridge.

111. *The Jets ride, introduced in 1958, was still thriving in the new decimal currency world of 1971.*

New brooms herald a new era

The new owners said their aim was to make Dreamland the finest amusement complex in the south of England. Within 12 months Phonographic announced a five year plan to make it one of the world's greatest parks, ready to spend £500,000 fulfilling that promise. At the same time it changed its name to Associated Leisure Entertainments Ltd.

112. *The Alice in Wonderland ride ran close to the Queen Mary replica.*

New managing director Douglas Harrison, previously a member of Dreamland's administrative staff who had joined as a cashier in 1946, was to oversee several radical departures from previous operating practices, as well as supervise almost as many changes as Margate had seen in its now lengthy history.

During that first year he and other senior managers travelled more than 40,000 miles seeking new ideas. They went to Germany, Spain and the United States, where they visited Disneyland and Las Vegas. While preserving the best of the old, the new owners set about their task with relish.

The cinema was rapidly becoming unprofitable, handicapped now by its 2,200 capacity. A few concerts by, among others Roy Orbison and Dorothy Squires, had proved outstandingly successful and this indicated a potential for live entertainment on a scale which had not previously been attempted. Accordingly in February 1973 the cinema closed, reopening at Easter with the circle attractively divided – at a cost of more than £55,000 – into two smaller

113. A scene from the controversial play The Bed while at the Royalty Theatre, London, which featured Jenny Kenna and John Higgins, prior to coming to Dreamland .

cinemas each seating 350. In the weeks after the opening movie fans were able to choose between seeing The Godfather, Treasure Island, MASH, Butch Cassidy & The Sundance Kid and the new release of James Bond in Live and Let Die.

With echoes of 1935, publicity material announced the new structure had called for 69 tons of timber, 25 tons of steel, 2.5 tons of nails, five tons of acoustic tiles and 20 tons of plaster board!

Seat prices were now 50p and 45p with reductions for children and OAPs. The cost included the newly introduced Value Added Tax.

The former stalls and stage now comprised the Dreamland Theatre where the curtain went up on The Dick Emery Show to a packed house.

A risqué comedy farce entitled The Bed, presented by Paul Raymond – owner of London's Raymond's Revue Bar and soft porn magazine Men Only – arrived for the summer season and immediately caused controversy.

It's fair to say Margate probably wasn't ready for a play featuring full frontal nudity – residents were suitably shocked and horrified. Despite the attendant

publicity, the production which starred John Inman, straight from TVs Are You Being Served, and six female co stars, played to less than full houses.

Dreamland's Fun Seekers newspaper said: "As the title of the play implies, the farce revolves around a bed, fitted with eccentric gadgetry, which is the proud possession of the central male character who can cause things to happen which give the young ladies in the play plenty to think about."

114. The Paratrooper ride in full swing during the 1970s.

115. A walk in the park in the 1970s – the fashions confirm why this was the decade good taste forgot.

Naughty but not obscene is how the the Isle of Thanet Gazette summed it up: "When one has had an eyeful of bottoms and bosoms it becomes a succession of comic seaside postcards brought to life. All naughty, clean fun without being obscene."

More family oriented entertainment was to be found in the Garden Café where trumpeter Ken Grieff and his trio held sway for a 10 week season until September.

In a June 1973 Dreamland press release Ken correctly observed there was quite a contrast in the kind of entertainment he offered from The Bed. "My audience is largely parents who bring their children for a night's music and sing song," he said.

The next summer season saw another farce No Sex Please We're British, grace the theatre's stage.

Jessie Matthews was to have taken the lead role here but fell ill before the 1974 run started and so was replaced by Pip Hinton. The company included Deal based Carry On actor Charles Hawtrey as well as Carol Hawkins and Peter Denyer who were appearing in TVs Fenn Street Gang at the time.

116. Charles Hawtrey, a regular of many Carry On films, was a star at Dreamland in 1974.

New brooms herald a new era

117. A view inside the new look bingo hall after conversion in the 1970s.

In 1973 the decision was taken to refurbish the ballroom and rename it The Topspot. After a two month long £30,000 restyling it opened with a concert by Georgie Fame followed the night after by The Tremeloes.

Billed as the most 'in' place in Kent for young people, it was equipped with nearly 1,000 lights connected by three miles of cable. More than 400 decorative lamps fixed to fade and flash were set under seating with another 400 in the stage wings able to colour pulse to sound. A projector threw patterns on the walls and stage while a second, fitted with a zoom lens, cast pictures on to a 26 feet wide screen.

One of the most successful events at Topspot was a concert by Rock & Roll King Bill Haley and the Comets who were beginning a 20th anniversary British tour in February 1974.

Rock Around The Clock, See You Later Alligator, Shake, Rattle and Roll, and Rip It Up featured that memorable night. Aside from Bill, then aged 47, the line up included two original Comets, Reynold Cawley on bass and Rudolph Pompili on saxophone.

Many of the audience came suitably dressed, men in long coats and drainpipe trousers and women in pencil skirts and fitted jackets. The happy audience included middle aged people but there were also many in their twenties too.

Topspot would see many big name groups during its four year life including The Drifters, Slade, The Marmalade, Suzi Quattro and Alvin Stardust.

118. The Astroglide became a firm favourite after its 1973 arrival – allegedly in lieu of a debt to Dreamland.

Back out in the park new rides were arriving such as 20,000 Leagues Under The Sea. Adapted freely from the Jules Verne tale, it was the first ride of its kind in the country and cost £25,000 to build. By hopping into one of the cars, passengers would be transported to Verne's undersea world, complete with true sound effects and full animation. They would ride through the belly of a whale, past Captain Nemo's machine room, watch an undersea ballet and ride on to the Lost City of Atlantis to be frightened by hordes of undersea spiders.

Another attraction which quickly became a favourite was the Astroglide. A six lane, undulating, 50 feet high slide, its polished plastic surface ensured fast riding – some of that actually spent airborne! – before landing among a heap of sprawling bodies at the bottom.

The River Caves Ride was given a much needed overhaul as it marked its 50th anniversary. During the work a teaspoon marked Wembley Exhibition 1924 was discovered in the structure.

The general state of the economy in the early 1970s made life difficult for most people and by

119. and 120. Crowds gathered to see Birdland in action and watch parrots riding bicycles.

now fewer staff were employed at the park. Before long nearly every Dreamland activity was being operated by a concessionaire – not only stalls and small rides but major rides and even the catering and cinema.

No longer able to retain about 15 of the 35 or so ride attendants to work on maintenance through the winter, a number of the long established rides were dismantled during the seventies and sold for little more than scrap value, among them the Racing Coaster – 50 years old and no longer a thriller, and the Miniature Railway, from which the surviving steam engine Billie – its companion Prince Edward having been disposed of in 1969 – was sold to the Marine Lake Railway, Rhyl, from where it originated.

Their replacements were complex, ultra modern rides such as the Orbiter, the Tip-Top and the Swirl whose maintenance was undertaken by their owners. These appealed to visitors but destroyed the even appearance of the park where the rides had always been surrounded by uniform wooden fences and lamp posts, set off by colourful flower beds and neatly trimmed hedges. At their peak, the gardeners were growing no less than 10,000 geraniums a year among many others, using three greenhouses located in the void space of the Scenic Railway.

A beer festival was held for the first time at Dreamland in 1972. This one day event proved such a success that it became a two day occasion the following year. The Garden Café rang to the sound of hundreds of clinking glasses as mighty thirsts were quenched that August. Four breweries were invited to ply their wares during the two days bringing with them traditional horse drawn drays which were paraded through the town. By the end some 900 gallons – or 7,200 pints – had been consumed and such was the event's popularity that beer festivals continued until 1978.

Thursday night fireworks displays discontinued at the end of the 1973 season. The final straw was the high investment which would be needed to replace the now worn out seating edging the car park arena. This brought an end to a tradition which had marked the opening of Dreamland park and celebrated everything including 50 years of Scouting, Margate's Borough Centenary, Victories at War and all the royal births, weddings and coronations. These events had been preceded by, in the thirties, a marching display by a leading military band and,

121. The Italian designed Cyclone cost £70,000 to install.

in the fifties, community singing with Margate Silver Band. It was temporarily replaced by a version of the It's A Knock Out television game.

On the plus side £70,000 was spent on the Cyclone, an exciting gravity ride of Italian design which was sited near the Scenic Railway – close to the spot previously occupied by the Racing Coaster.

Despite earlier plans to make Dreamland one of the world's best, there was now a creeping reluctance to continue investing in Margate, seen as a declining holiday town. Cheap foreign holidays had markedly reduced the appeal and contributed to the vicious circle of fewer amenities, falling visitor numbers and anti-social behaviour by drunken teenagers.

However, Associated Leisure decided to make its first ever investment in a sporting activity by spending £40,000 on the latest squash playing trend. In July 1977, four courts and a gymnasium were officially opened in the former Topspot by Kent and England cricketer Derek Underwood. This soon built up a club membership of 700. Two of the squash courts were glass fronted and a viewing gallery gave spectators the chance to see championship games.

Members were drawn from across East Kent competing in a number of local leagues. Increasing demand among players and beginners led to two more courts being added three years later as well as a small sports shop. These occupied the space taken by the gymnasium which transferred to the basement of the Tivoli Leisure Centre in Marine Terrace. The squash club would last for another 10 years, until November 1990, when falling membership made it no longer viable.

122. The gym formed an initial part of the squash club.

New brooms herald a new era

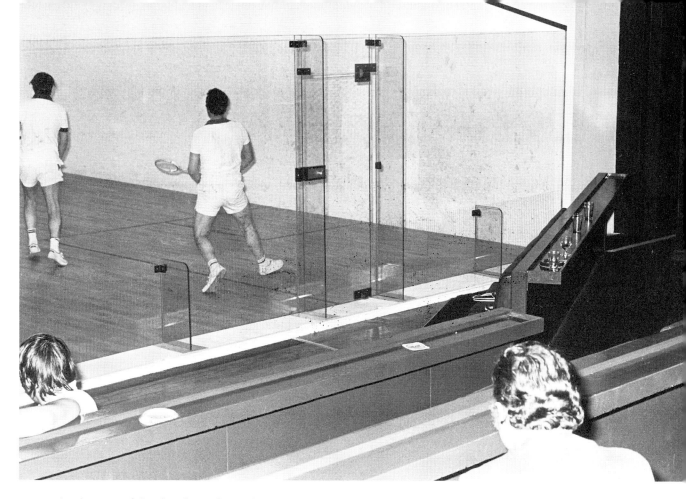

123. *A view into one of the glass fronted squash courts, taken in the late 1970s.*

Outdoors, the Water Chute was proving its worth. Installed in 1977, there were only four in Britain at the time. The others were at Blackpool, Rhyl and Porthcawl, where the ride was first introduced by inventor, Sir Leslie Joseph, in the mid thirties. A shareholder in Margate Estates in the 1950s, he supervised installation at Dreamland where it was operated as a joint venture with his company, Trust House Forte Leisure Ltd.

The ride had in fact been reconstituted from a partly burnt out one from Battersea Fun Fair. The six cars each carrying six passengers dropped from 50 feet into a 13,000 gallon tank of water, reaching a speed of around 45 miles per hour. The Cyclone ride was moved later to another area of the park to make way for the Water Chute.

1977 also saw the removal of the Sky Wheel, two big wheels in one, which Jack Lynch had designed and built at Dreamland in 1953. The Sky Wheel was bought by a Dutch operator and shipped to Holland with Britain's only other example which came from Great Yarmouth, for a total of £12,000. This was a bargain price considering the Margate ride alone had cost £17,500 to build.

124. **The Water Chute made a big splash from 1977.**

125. Large model dinosaurs roamed the park in the 1970s. This publicity photo shows one being offered a glass of beer during the 1974 beer festival.

Any fears of Dreamland becoming a remote outpost of a large company were quashed at the beginning of 1975 when Associated Leisure formed a new division at Margate to coordinate its rapidly expanding activities. From its HQ, senior management oversaw operations at centres in Berwick-on-Tweed to the Isle of Wight and from Liverpool to Weymouth. This arrangement would last until 1980.

At this time, the Safari Zoo having undergone various unsuccessful phases, including a Parrot Jungle and a Monster Park, with half life size fibreglass reproductions of prehistoric creatures, was revamped as Magicland in 1980 in an attempt to recreate the success of the Magic Garden. Many of its set pieces had been stored but had either deteriorated or were considered too old fashioned to reuse. A new set of fairytale scenes, illuminated at night was constructed but made little impact.

126. A Mister Man welcomes visitors to Magicland in 1980.

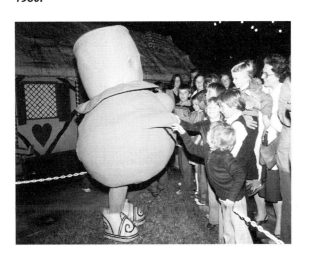

127. A new dodgem track arrived in 1978.

128. Lena Blair, left, and Miss Cheeta tussle during their bout in the Garden Café in 1978.

The latter part of the decade saw the park being given something of a facelift, notably with the removal in 1977 of the Queen Mary centrepiece to help widen the entrance to the main attractions. In its place went 14 sideshows and a new dodgem car track.

The Garden Café hosted a summer season of weekly wrestling competitions for the first time in 1978 arranged by professional TV wrestler Jackie Pallo. The opening contest in July was a best selling success between him and lithe Jon Cortez but the limelight was taken by a ladies' contest between the well-built Miss Lena Blair and the slender Miss Cheeta. Eager crowds shouted their support and after a hectic tussle Miss Lena defeated her opponent by one fall and one submission to one fall.

129. A long time family favourite, the antique Gallopers roundabout was taken out of the park in 1980.

130. The helter skelter was still going strong as the park marked its golden jubilee.

131. Advertising manager Mick Tomlinson made scale models of the park's rides. Here he shows off his version of the Big Wheel with daughter Clare in 1980.

1980 was the park's golden jubilee year and more attractions arrived now to help mark the event. A fond farewell was bade to Doug Harrison in February when he retired after no less than 35 years working for Dreamland, the last nine as MD. He had certainly seen the best of years at the park and like John Henry and Eric Iles had given his all to its continued success. Harrison died in 1987 aged 68.

Numerous events and promotions offering discounted fares or free rides were held throughout the summer.

Among the publicity Dreamland's jubilee attracted was a celebratory supplement in the amusement trade newspaper World's Fair. On the back page of this editorial, a representative speaking for the Kent & Sussex section of the fairground concessionaires professional body said: "The park is still showing itself as the leader in this part of the country. There can be no doubt that Dreamland must play a major role in the general economy of the Thanet area.

"It attracts huge numbers of visitors, who of course, spend vast sums of money throughout the area – and not just at the amusement park alone."

These words were spoken by one who would later take on the mantle of Dreamland ownership – one Jimmy Godden.

What was probably the biggest ride of them all turned up in golden jubilee year in the guise of the 148 feet high Big Wheel. This was added at a cost of £150,000, rotating up to 240 riders in its gondolas for a thrilling aerial view of Margate and was itself visible for miles around.

132. Tony Blackburn inspects the complete model with Mick at a show in 1976.

133. The biggest of Big Wheels, at nearly 150 feet high, made its Dreamland debut in 1980. Thrilling views for all were guaranteed.

134. A youthful Jim Davidson made a guest appearance to promote the Newice rink in 1980.

Unfortunately, the other main venture marking the park's jubilee would prove a distinct failure – the installation of a synthetic ice skating rink, Newice, in the old Garden Café. Intended as a year round facility, 500 sq metres of polyethylene blocks of Newice were laid following encouragement by the local council. Key users were meant to be schools and youth clubs just as much as residents and visitors. One of only two in the country, it opened halfway through Dreamland's golden jubilee year at a cost of £150,000 but survived for only 15 loss-making months by which time less than 200 people were using it at weekends.

Indeed, there was a feeling among some staff that the Newice rink was never really meant to make a profit – merely just appear as a useful asset for any new owner in the event of a sale.

Whether or not it made any difference at all is unknown but in May 1981 Associated Leisure announced it had sold the freehold of Dreamland for £1.6 million to the Dutch amusement park operators, the Bembom family.

135. In 1980 sultry sisters Julie, left, and Dawn Stevens, variously Miss Broadstairs and Miss Margate, were also invited to try out the rink. Hopefully, it was a warm day.

New brooms herald a new era

136. *Willem, left, and Mathys Bembom took over running the park and are pictured in front of the new Ladybird ride in March 1982, just before opening for their first full season.*

To the Millennium – and beyond?

The Bembom family already ran the Ponypark Holiday centre at Slagharen, in northern Holland, as well as two smaller parks – one near Marseilles and the other at Kirchhorst near Hanover.

The family's purchase of Dreamland was completed by November 1981 and two of the seven brothers, Willem and Mathys, sons of Hank, were put in charge working with general manager Alan Coppin who had succeeded Doug Harrison.

The Bembom Brothers were quick to realise that major changes to the park were necessary, both in terms of what it offered visitors and its own public image.

For a long time Dreamland had been tarnished by regular problems of drunken behaviour, vandalism and fighting. One of the first moves was to change the name to Bembom Brothers Theme Park. This didn't apply to the cinemas as they had been leased to another operator by Associated Leisure and so both names could be clearly seen adorning the skyscraper building.

Bembom's other parks operated by charging an admission fee, allowing visitors free access to all the rides. It was proposed to introduce this to Margate. For the princely sum of £2.50, the whole park was yours for the day. There was some local scepticism about such a scheme but the Bemboms correctly assessed that a controlled admission system, with potential trouble makers barred, would encourage business.

Since alcohol contributed to the disorders of the past, the bars around the park were closed, and this applied to the seafront buildings which were leased back to Associated Leisure. The Bemboms also abandoned evening opening – closing at 6pm – thus not only making

137. The cinema building bearing both Dreamland and Bembom Brothers signage in the late 1980s.

considerable savings in power and wages, but also avoiding vandalism which had become a serious problem after dark. In any case, most visitors to Margate were day trippers who started leaving for home in the early evening.

Operation of the rides and sideshows was taken back by the Bemboms with the concessionaires, naturally disgruntled, being told to remove their equipment. This would be gradually replaced by impressive thrill rides such as the Looping Star from Germany whose cars looped the loop, a replica of the Mary Rose which carried 40 passengers through a complete orbit and a swinging Pirate Ship, which merely travelled through 180 degrees!

The Wave Swinger, a gigantic Chair-o-Plane whose central stem moved, was installed for the

138. The Pirate Ship, Hanseatic, came complete with German signage upon its arrival in Margate. It was able to replicate sailing in a force 12 gale.

139. *The German made Looping Star combined with the Big Wheel to make a dramatic impact on the park's skyline when it arrived for the 1982 season.*

140. *The Mary Rose was able to traverse through 360 degrees – for anyone who had the stomach for it.*

To the Millennium – and beyond?

141. The Meteor gravity ride was another of the new additions to Margate during the 1980s.

1984 season. This increased the number of rides to around 30 which now spread on to the coach park. The nearby former Margate station goods yard was bought for £125,000 to provide extra parking.

Even small children benefited from modern rides, including a little motor cycle track with 10 mini Yamaha bikes. The whole park was also completely resurfaced.

Bringing this new lease of life to Dreamland was fully justified in the first few seasons with attendances of nearly two million a year. The one price concept spread to other British amusement parks whose operators could see improved cash control, security and far simpler administration.

Among the millions now visiting Dreamland were thousands of Arabs arriving from London in large chauffeur driven limousines. To encourage them further, the brothers decided a grassy 80 sq yard area of the park should be set aside to enable them to pray facing Mecca.

General manager Alan Coppin told the Thanet Times in August 1984: "Some wear Western clothes and many are accompanied by their wives in full yashmaks. They enjoy the thrills and excitement because there is nothing like this in the Middle East.

"We are now considering how we can serve the

142. The Ladybird, a modern roller coaster for kids, in action at the end of the 1990s.

Arabs better and are thinking of introducing a kebab restaurant as well as the private area where they can make their devotions to Mecca. It can be a bit embarrassing for them in the middle of the park

"We are anxious to cater for their needs, but we don't want to upset people nor do we want it all to be a joke."

Nonetheless, a Thanet Council spokesman was quoted in the Daily Mail, who picked up on the story, saying Margate would now have to swop its beach donkeys for camels.

1985 saw the Golden Jubilee of the cinema's opening and was celebrated in style with the return of Lewis Gerard from his home in Santa Barbara, California, to play the Compton organ one more time.

Lewis flew into a British winter from an 87 degree climate in the US and promptly caught a chill. Swift action with a visit to a local chemist saved the day and Lewis was able to play a two hour concert suitably decongested.

Fully restored variously by the Medway and Margate Theatre Organ Clubs, the Compton

excited all who attended this special event. Lewis paid tribute to those who had looked after the organ saying it had played 1,000 times better than in 1935. Lewis visited Dreamland again in 1994 before dying the following year aged 84.

143. Another youngsters' ride was the Big Apple.

144. Not a new ride by any means, the Waltzer was still wowing its customers in the late 1990s.

New attractions came and went in the park. Two of the most notable farewells were those of the River Caves and the neighbouring Sphinx in 1984. Rising maintenance costs and the pressing need for something new combined to see them off. Sadly, both attractions were simply demolished with no attempt made to salvage any of their more evocative components.

Continuing the trend to cater for younger children as well as adults, other arrivals in the 1980s included the Ladybird – a twisty, turning roller ride with cars painted like the black and red insect – and the Enterprise, with its suspended cars swinging through 180 degrees. For those preferring to keep their feet firmly on the ground, the 3-D Cinema 2000 provided thrills in a large orange and white tent showing car chases spliced with sequences from white knuckle rides.

The Bembom brothers kept the park in good shape and succeeded in giving it a much needed new perception in the view of the paying public and it had rightly become one of the 10 most visited tourist attractions in the UK by the late 1980s.

145. The Sphinx was a fixture for many years, only disappearing in the 1980s.

But the Dreamland name wouldn't go away – somehow telling friends you were going to Bembom's never did sound particularly exciting – and so the old name was reintroduced in 1990 to local delight. By now it cost £5.99 each to enjoy the rides.

The Sunshine Room in the cinema building now became Coco's children's indoor play park, with lots of climbing equipment and multi-coloured ball ponds. It proved an ideal place for youngsters to enjoy an afternoon, especially if going for a birthday party. Below it, the former Bali Hai bar was turned into an arcade, which it remains today.

Greenery was once again recognised as an important ingredient in making the park a cheerful place. Frank Buttery, a long serving employee who had become operations manager, was able to tell the Isle of Thanet Gazette in 1993 that more vegetation would make a pleasant change to the drab concrete which proliferated. Early on that year he said they had already planted 25 additional trees and extra flower beds.

Return to Bemboms' of the cinema building's lease in 1992 prompted an extensive refurbishment programme. Nearly £400,000 was spent on transforming the 850 seat bingo hall into one of the most luxurious of its kind in the county. Keeping faith with the past, the scheme attempted to retain the original art deco atmosphere alongside new seats, carpets and computerised electronics.

Happily, two statues dating back to the building's Hall By The Sea days were uncovered, restored and placed on either side of the stage to gaze down upon the players.

The management also took the chance to add a small dance floor in front of the caller's podium to use during tea dances which were being reintroduced at the time with the idea that music would be provided by the Compton organ.

As Steven Spielberg's dinosaur epic Jurassic Park was released so a year long programme to refurbish the cinemas was completed in 1993. This £200,000 transformation took a long time to finish because the cinemas remained open throughout the work. It was the first time they had been upgraded on such a scale since twinning in the 1970s. Acres of new carpet were

146. Stomach churning rides like this helped draw considerable numbers during the 1990s.

fitted along with a computerised ticket system and a cosy bar. A new Dolby stereo sound system was added as well.

To celebrate the occasion 14 films were shown non stop in one day for just 99 pence. One couple got their money's worth seeing them all running from 10am to close down at 11.30pm! Jurassic Park incidentally showed to packed houses during a four week spell in the summer.

In 1995, Dreamland was 75 years old and the all wooden Scenic Railway went into the Guinness Book of Records as the oldest roller coaster in the country. Some refurbishment work was carried out around the park's entrance tunnel at the beginning of what was planned to be another gradual redevelopment programme. This was also the year free admission returned to the park with the rides categorised according to age or height suitability.

More and more people were finding fixed entry price becoming expensive, admitted managing director Bob de Boer, especially if some members

147. The Wild Mouse was introduced to Margate in the late 1990s and caused a sensation among eager visitors.

of the family or group didn't want to go on very many rides.

The return of free admission saw Bemboms' management buying neighbouring businesses, including the Cinque Ports pub on the opposite side of Hall By The Sea Road.
This plan had cost £1 million itself and the park improvements would add another £500,000.

But by the end of this year the Bemboms sold Dreamland on to established arcade and fairground owner Jimmy Godden. He owned the Rotunda amusement park in Folkestone as well as numerous arcades there and in Thanet and Dover.

Bought for an undisclosed sum, further development of the park was assisted by a £450,000 grant from the Single Regeneration Budget – European money awarded to areas in need of improvement – while Thanet District Council chipped in with another £50,000.

One of the new rides introduced in the late 1990s was the Wild Mouse, a large yellow metal structure with a series of four seater cars taking their passengers on a seemingly hazardous roller

coaster ride. With sharp turns and sudden drops now typifying modern attractions, it was a far cry from the Scenic Railway.

At the same time, in 1997, the Big Wheel, now as much a landmark of Dreamland as the cinema building, was taken down and sold to an amusement park in Mexico City. It was a long job. Dismantling the wheel, its gondolas and the massive supports took 10 days when only three were scheduled. Eventually, it was carried off in three lorry loads to the Isle of Grain for shipment to Mexico.

Dreamland saw the arrival of the new Millennium with more cash spent on refurbishment and the return of the Looping Star ride.

In January 2001 the Isle of Thanet Gazette announced that Jimmy Godden's company was negotiating with a leading supermarket, thought to be Morrisons, to sell some of the park's land for a new store. While true, the talks eventually came to nothing.

By now it was plain to see for even the most casual observer that things were not what they were

in the park. Large open spaces were appearing where there had previously been rides and the overall impression was one of a lack of tender, loving care, despite substantial investment.

Considering this, it was perhaps not surprising to learn that visitor numbers were falling. Despite widespread positive publicity when the Scenic Railway was given Grade II listing in March 2002 – the only amusement park ride in the country to be accorded this status – Jimmy Godden's company announced at the beginning of 2003 the park might close forever at the end of the summer season and be redeveloped into shops and leisure units by the Stadium Group.

148. Even as it was being dismantled, the Big Wheel looked imposing.

To the Millennium – and beyond?

149. Clear track ahead – a front seat view on the now grade two listed Scenic Railway in 2003.

It appears that, at best, a much scaled down amusement park could be retained and stay open for business in 2004.

As we write, there is still a lot of uncertainty but a strong Save Dreamland Campaign has been formed to prevent closure and has gained no less than 13,000 supporters from far and near. The campaign has won a great deal of media coverage, has been lobbying decision makers and holding regular meetings with leaders at Thanet District Council.

Campaign mastermind Nick Laister, an

150. Although weathered, the 1935 building still manages to look impressive for visitors to Margate.

Oxfordshire based planning consultant and amusement park preservationist, found a French operator willing to take over the park and has won support from Thanet District Council, rightly worried that Margate's tourist trade would evaporate without it.

The campaign also worked closely with a specially formed trust to ensure the Scenic Railway could continue to run during 2003. After essential maintenance, the ride was running by mid May as a separate concession from the rest of the park. The other rides had earlier been leased by Jimmy Godden to showman David Wallis for the season.

To the Millennium – and beyond?

151. *The Clifton Baths Estate as it looked in the early 1920s, soon after purchase by John Henry Iles.*

A leisurely life at the Lido

Where Dreamland was mainly designed for the kiss me quick, squeeze me slow day tripper, so the Lido, just a mile up the road in Cliftonville, was aimed at a more select class of visitor staying in the area for a week or two.

John Henry Iles realised quite early on this was a market which needed to be catered for. Shortly after getting Dreamland up and running in 1920 he bought the Clifton Baths Estate, a genteel sort of place which could trace its origins back a further 100 years when it had been frequented by the 'nobility and gentry resorting to Margate'. The estate was especially well known to generations for its hot salt water baths.

Its links with the past were many. Great caverns, honeycombed with passages, had been cut into the cliffs and once offered a hiding place to local smugglers. These were the result of many hours hard labour which were sometimes ill rewarded. One gang made the mistake of burrowing too far upwards and found themselves in the kitchen of the revenue officer's cottage!

When Iles purchased the estate, it came complete with a funicular cliff railway, which had been installed just before the First World War, a cinema and the Joywheel ride. This was soon transferred to Dreamland and renamed the Lunar Ride.

152. *An engraving of the Clifton baths dating from 1824.*

153. How the Clifton Baths Estate looked in a drawing from 1927 soon after the swimming pool's completion.

In the years that followed, Iles spent £120,000 improving and rebuilding the estate with a cliff top sun terrace, bandstand and bars spread over three levels. An indoor warm sea water pool was the only one in Thanet, open from Easter to October and 'constantly attended by a highly skilled instructor'.

154. The funicular railway or cliff lift dated from 1913.

By 1925 Iles had leased a stretch of the foreshore from Margate Corporation and had embarked on a £60,000 programme to build a vast open air swimming pool.

The pool would be big enough to accommodate nearly 1,000 swimmers, with changing rooms and plenty of space for sitting, sunbathing and enjoying drinks afterwards – exactly what the paying public now wanted.

At 250 feet by 150 feet and depth graduating from two feet in the shallows to nine feet, sea water was drawn in through four large sluices at high tides. Around 1,300 tons of cement and 10,000 tons of ballast were used to construct the pool. Some 3,000 people could sit and enjoy the antics from terraced seating – or amphitheatre as it was properly known – set into the cliff edge. Close by, there was a huge dressing room with 400 changing cubicles. This was later extended to 800 with plunge, shower and foot baths.

A young girl was ceremoniously pushed into the pool as the first swimmer at the official opening by the Mayor of Margate, Cllr Mrs MHS Hatfeild, on 24 June 1927 – immediately followed by a typical British summer drenching which saw the entire party adjourn to the new French themed Normandie Cafe for an early lunch.

155. Early bathing belles were happy to pose for the camera in 1927 – much to the amusement of the lads nearby.

Later, three maroons were fired over the pool – for the King, the Mayor and Margate. This was followed by an exhibition of diving, boxing and wrestling on rafts by local clubs and a life saving display from the local police.

For years after the pool would be open for much of the day during the summer season, closing at around midnight after evenings of moonlit swimming with appropriate mood

156. Painting commemorating the pool's opening. The original hung in centre manager Arthur Ashwood's office for many years.

music. The Clifton Baths changed its name to the Lido in 1938, prompting one of those awkward unknowns – should it be pronounced Leedo or Liedo? Various dictionaries suggest the former but to this day, you can hear both uttered in any conversation about the place.

The story of Margate is closely linked with that of the seaside resort concept, the town becoming one of the first to allow mixed sea bathing in 1907. It also became one of the cradles of the beauty contest idea back in the thirties – thanks to the weekly events held at the Clifton Baths new pool.

It was a hot summer in 1930 when the first contests were held, bursting on to a public already becoming captivated by Hollywood glamour and the first talkies.

The earliest competitors were mainly parades of girl holidaymakers who entered for a lark and were delighted if they came away with a box of chocolates.

Compere at those early beauty parades was Eric Iles, who had graduated from Oxford and would eventually become Dreamland's chairman and managing director. It was not until much later that

157. Show a leg – fragile showcards thought to date from the early thirties advertising the Clifton's virtues.

158. Glamour photo of young girls on a pool slide.

bathing costumes became a thing of fashion, he recalled in the 1960s. Many of the contestants hired swimsuits for use at the pool, either from the baths or the nearby FL Pettman's bathing station at Newgate Gap.

Woollen, in a standard blue with the pool's name emblazoned across the front, they did little to advance the female form. The only thing different about them was the sizes – large, medium and small. On the other hand the top prizes were bathing costumes presented by a well known manufacturer.

By now women were no longer afraid of showing an ankle at the seaside and the contests were considered modern. In those early years, said Iles, more girls entered and 50 at a time was no exception, whereas later they became competition conscious, concerned about general standards of beauty, while some felt they could not compete against prettier faces, or those with striking figures.

Judges changed over time too. Before the second world war they were nearly always women – three would be invited from the audience, but it was found women were too analytical. After 1945 judges were almost always men and there would often be a showbiz personality on hand as well to decide the winners.

159. *Leisurely times at the Cliff Café sun terrace. Alfresco sun lounging or, in the evening, somewhere to cool off.*

160. *Staying in the shade, albeit on a diving board.*

The beauty contests developed and, week by week, they featured different aspects of female charm.

Typical titles for contests were Miss Physical Excellence, Miss Calf and Ankle, Miss Lovely Legs, Miss Sports Girl, Miss Mermaid and Miss Grace and Bearing. Later on Miss South Seas Siren was another title.

The organisers found if girls wore ballet type skirts over costumes they could be opened to enable judges to concentrate on legs without being influenced by pretty faces. In some contests girls actually wore hoods over their faces, giving them a Ku Klux Klan appearance!

Poise and colour could be achieved by handing girls soldier type hats with a drum major's stick for the leader. Adding spectacle and balance, girls in the Grace and Bearing contest were handed Grecian urns with which to parade around the pool. Vital statistics were the vogue of the beauty parade too but there is no record of the measurements of the first girl to win at the Lido. In those far off days no one dared to ask!

161. *Swimwear was more flattering to the figure by the 1950s. Any bets on the young lady fourth from left winning?*

162. *An unusual shot from 1938 of a Miss Lovely Legs contest where competitors had to turn and show an ankle.*

A leisurely life at the Lido

163. *Not all poolside activities called for beauty. A little muscle helped from time to time as well.*

164. *More competitors line up for a parade in 1951.*

165. All smiles for Miss South Seas Siren winners – sensible grass skirts supplied – after receiving their prizes in 1957.

166. Right, the one wearing the flat cap is Bill Maynard, posing with entrants in the Miss Avro contest in 1965.

167. Below, slipping into something a little fishy are these three winners of a Miss Mermaid event in 1959.

During the 1960s a few large companies would arrange their own contests from among their female employees with finals held at places such as the Lido – hence we have the Miss Avro girls in 1965 posing with Bill Maynard, latterly of ITV's Heartbeat fame, who was star of the theatre's main show that year.

Later on, Lido contests were supported by tobacco manufacturer Rothman's who, in the early 1970s, held a gala day there with its own flying aerobatic team passing overhead for a half hour long display. How tastes have changed – smoking sponsorship has been outlawed and beauty parades are considered politically incorrect.

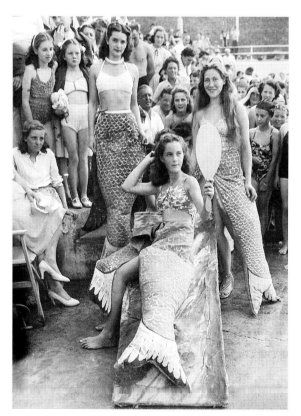

168. *The pool was in good order when this aerial view of the Lido was captured in the 1950s.*

169. *The high diving boards have been put to good use for this 1950s group photo.*

170. Inside the 1,500 seat theatre. Note how the sunlight shines through the open roof.

Meanwhile on top of the cliffs, there emerged a giant new theatre for 1930. With seating for 1,500 and a sliding roof which would be opened during show intervals, it became a renowned venue on the summer show circuit, giving many up and coming performers an invaluable chance to hone their skills.

The theatre replaced the old cinema which was a wooden building dating back to 1910 and had opened originally as the Electric Theatre before becoming the Clifton Cinema. An advertisement in the town guide of 1911 boasts: 'Latest films – Continuous show – Programme changed daily'. Selections of music were played on the latest concert gramophone equipment – usually the

Grenadier and Coldstream guards – during the intervals. Seat prices for adults were 6d and 3d and children were admitted for 3d and 2d each.

Publicity for the cinema in 1912 announced it was: 'The only theatre in Thanet using the stereoscopic screen, assuring steadiness and brilliancy' and by 1920 boasted: 'A fine new sunbrite screen, the largest and brightest pictures in town'.

The Clifton cinema was a popular venue for around 20 years but didn't survive the death blow dealt by the arrival of talking pictures. A decision was taken not to wire it for sound, leaving manager Jack Binns who also managed Dreamland's cinema, with only one venue to promote.

A leisurely life at the Lido

171. *The gentlemen's hairdressing salon of the Clifton Baths soon after completion in the early 1930s.*

Also during the early 1930s ladies and gentlemen's hairdressing salons were constructed along this top level nearest the Ethelbert Crescent side. Ladies were assured: 'Specialist staff have been engaged from leading establishments, highly skilled in all branches of the profession, including permanent waving.'

For the men, no expense had been spared in making their salon the finest and best equipped in the district. Comfort and cleanliness were everywhere in evidence, promotional brochures insisted.

172. *The main entrance to the Lido in 1947, clearly showing the front of the theatre.*

173. **The Cliff Café ready for visitors in 1935. It was expanded to accommodate 1,000 people.**

174. **Cliff Café 'nippies' adorn the newly created bandstand in 1937.**

175. A corner of the Jolly Tar Tavern in the mid 1930s. A nautical style welcome awaited willing customers.

Nearby were 50 private bathrooms serving medical and hot sea water baths. Each one had been fitted with marble floors and walls while the ozone filled waters 'continually helped cure rheumatism, sciatica and nervous disorders'. These would feature at the Lido at least until the outbreak of war.

An aquarium and mini zoo would replace the baths in the immediate post war era and survive for much of the 1950s. Filled with exotic tropical and coldwater fish plus a host of reptiles, and

even a few monkeys, this attraction was spread out on two levels. Among the keepers who cared for the animals was Gerald Durrell, later a famed naturalist, author and founder in 1959 of the Jersey Zoo. He was a relief keeper in 1951.

The bars were given a makeover during the 1930s. All had a theme of one kind or another. Largest was the Cliff Café. Originally designed to accommodate just 80 people in the early 1920s, it was extended to seat 1,000 in comfort. It provided an ideal vantage point from which to

176. The aquarium frontage soon after opening in 1948.

177. Dancing the night away on the Sun Terrace in 1950.

enjoy the sea views and pool scenes. Orchestras would play throughout the day and night.

The Café Normandie was decorated after the old style of the French region and was home to various orchestras for dancing during the thirties. The idea of something French, foreign and therefore immediately exciting was carried through to the French bar on the swimming pool level. Murals recalled the days of pirates on the high seas while the bar stools were made from the screws of old French wine presses.

Seafaring was more prominent in the Jolly Tar tavern where lobster pot lampshades jostled with oddments of ships' running and fishing gear. Typically, the Foc'sle Accordion Entertainers would be on hand to supply the nautical music.

Underneath the Café Normandie was the Café Basque, which at the time was thought to be the only one of its kind. This had been modelled on bars found in the Basque region in the Pyrenees. Rustic treatment of wood beams and stone arches helped build the intimate atmosphere.

The 1930s settled into a happy pattern of music in the square bandstand on the top level terrace – enjoyed from the comparative comfort of a deck chair – swimming in the pool and a show at night. Occasionally John Henry Iles, dressed in plus fours, could be seen emerging from his Bentley to buy an ice cream and then

enthusiastically pretend to conduct the band.

Among the first of many seasonal delights to come to the Clifton was On With The Show presented by Lawrence Wright and featuring a cast of singers, dancers and a principal comedian – a formula that was typical of pre-television era summer shows around the country.

Although the performers were the same every night, their offerings were not. It was quite common for half a dozen versions of the programme to be produced setting out the changing bill – ideal for anyone staying in town to see something different every night of their holiday if they chose.

178. The then unique Café Basque cabaret bar.

A leisurely life at the Lido

By the mid 1930s the Cliff Theatre was venue of the nightly Gay Parade shows, produced initially by Richard Jerome. Clearly, one couldn't give a show this title now – but these were more innocent times and the word gay meant fun. The Six Dancing Debutantes propped up the bill of soprano and soubrette singers, two comedians and a general entertainer, all supported by The Parade Orchestra.

During these years immediately before the Second World War, one of the stars to appear here was Leslie Fuller. He was a fine example of local boy makes good. Born in Margate he once helped his father print papers and then sold them on the street. During the 1914-18 war he served with the Huntingdonshire Cycling Battalion, having been posted to this unit because of his records and championships obtained for cycle racing. He later formed a concert party, the Ped'lers, which met with great success in the Army.

He returned to Margate in 1919 and set up the concert party in a tent adjoining the site. Later on, the troupe moved in to the Clifton Concert

179. A 1938 handbill for Cabaret Revels. Note the use of the Lido Theatre name for the first time.

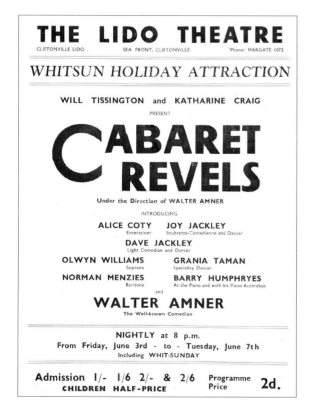

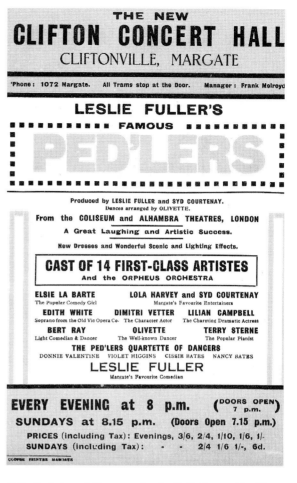

180. Early handbill promoting Leslie Fuller and Ped'lers.

Hall, now part of the Iles owned estate.

Throughout the 1920s and early 1930s Leslie Fuller and the Ped'lers were a familiar part of the estate. His talent for comedy took him on to films, making a total of 14 between 1930 and 1942. In 1934 the local papers reported he had signed a contract with one studio for £20,000 over five years.

Fatefully, in the late 1930s he set up a film production company with John Henry Iles as Chairman, based at Cricklewood in North London. This was the venture which would lead to Iles eventual financial downfall.

Leslie's antics were followed by Lido audiences for years and the Pedlers became one of Britain's best known concert parties. After 1945 he returned to Margate and became a local councillor. He also went back to the Lido for the 1947 season but was taken ill during the run and replaced by comedian Neville Kennard. The following year, still under 60, Leslie died.

181. *Reg Varney was a hit of the post war era. The picture shows him as himself, left, and as his own ventriloquist's dummy.*

In 1948 Hedley Claxton's Gaytime was presented in the theatre for the first time, running for the three seasons until 1950. Despite the austerity period, it was a more sophisticated show than the concert party style productions of earlier years. They are notable now in that two then rising comedians appeared on the bills. Topping the line up was Reg Varney, later to be better known in TVs On The Buses. One national newspaper critic observed Reg was getting 'something like a Danny Kaye reception'.

'Reg Varney is a chirpy little cockney with long, lank, reddish hair, a Joe E Brown grin, a Bob Hope nose and a pair of impish eyes', wrote Cecil Wilson in the Daily Mail.

For two of these three seasons, 1948 and 1950, one of the supporting artistes was a talented comedian who would also become famous on TV – Benny Hill. Arguably, Benny went on to become more widely known internationally as his shows would be – and still are – among the few which have been successful in America.

182. *A youthful Benny Hill appeared with Reg Varney in the Gaytime shows of 1948 and 1950.*

183. Just a small section of the damage caused by the storm in 1953. There was damage on all levels of the Lido.

Seat prices for 1950, including entertainment tax, were 4/6d down to 3/6d, 2/6d and 1/6d. Or in today's money, 23p, 17p, 13p, and 7p!

The Lido suffered severely in the 1953 storm which lashed most of the east coast. The swimming pool, at the mercy of the raging waves, was extensively damaged. So was the promenade and the adjoining buildings. The Café Normandie, opposite the pool entrance was wrecked when a 20ft slab of concrete hurtled into it. The café was not rebuilt.

184. Huge waves engulf the Lido pool during the 1953 storm. Happily, repairs were completed in time for the summer.

185. Above, Sherriff Arnold and fans demonstrate their speed on the draw in the 1960s. Chances are the girls were winners in that week's pool parade.

REGULAR DEPUTY SHERIFF OF BEXAR COUNTY, SAN ANTONIO.

In its place emerged the Golden Garter Saloon which was, for many summers after, the home of a Wild West type show.

Until the end of the 1960s this featured Sheriff Danny Arnold, show girls and a group of entertainers collectively known as the Vigilantes. Loud music, singing, the occasional shooting, a fully stocked bar and a jailhouse for the particularly unruly – as much the cast as the paying audience – made this a memorable night out for many.

Danny really was a sheriff – he was a deputy of Bexar County, San Antonio, Texas, and more than once helped out his American bosses by following up leads in Britain.

It was said the Canadian born wild west expert got an income tax allowance for cigars which were all part of his professional image and he paid half a guinea each for the five cigars he smoked a day.

Ever the entertainer, he could never resist ending even the most casual of conversations with a quip such as: "Look out for those injuns!"

186. Danny lights up one of his tax deductible cigars.

187. *The Sherriff, his Wild West Vigilantes and showgirls pose in the Golden Garter saloon in 1959.*

188. *The saloon's interior included a jail house and a set of gallows to quell the unruly element!*

189. The Lido was packed on all levels to watch a beauty contest in the 1960s.

190. Make It Tonight was the name of 1961's Lido show.

Making his mark with a new type of summer production, was Bunny Baron, who until his death in 1978 directed shows throughout the country. Lido Theatre audiences of the early fifties were able to see the quick speaking Londoner in the rollicking 'Sunshine and Smiles' for five seasons.

A period in which formal dress declined, it was all the more notable when worn. One man who gave a touch of the old days to Lido audiences was front of house manager Huntley Macdonald. A former professional actor, he was always to be seen wearing his dress suit, with neat red rose in the lapel, as customers were shown to their seats. Starting at the Lido just after the Second World War, Mac, as he was known, continued into the mid 1950s.

Similar format shows continued after Bunny left, and by the early sixties stars whose names were already made were shining at the Lido Theatre.

They included Beryl Reid, 1960, Bill Maynard, 1961 and 1965, while the 1964 season starred Tommy Trinder. His ad-libbing skills were thoroughly tested on opening night. The organ had broken down putting the musical part of the

191. Undated photo of dancers from the summer show.

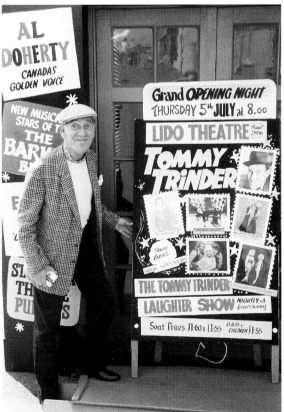

show out of action while repairs were hurriedly carried out, leaving Tommy jesting on stage by himself for 35 minutes. The audience, none the wiser, assumed it was all part of his act.

Shows with a similar music plus comedy format continued for several years but the public appeared to be growing tired of the type of production they could see on TV. The management decided on a change so comedy plays took over for a couple of years, then a colourful Carnival on Ice show in 1973. For this, the entire stage was taken up by a newly built ice tank which would take 18 hours to freeze over before it could be skated upon.

In 1974 there was a return to musical with 'The Amazing Penny Whistle Show' and a similar format was kept for 1975 but with Norman Wisdom as the star. This was a particularly good season for the Lido and house full boards were outside the theatre on many nights.

192. Tommy Trinder made a welcome return visit to the Lido Theatre for the 1979 summer season.

193. Norman Wisdom and show promoter Martin Gates celebrate a full house in 1975.

194. Charlie Drake gets the bird – 18 year old Elaine that is.

The following year comic Charlie Drake made a return from performing exile after a dispute with actor's union Equity. His 11 week season began in July and not long after he made national headlines when he announced his engagement to 18 year old chorus girl, Elaine Bird. The happy couple though did not marry. Appearing on the same bill was ventriloquist Roger de Courcey and his bear Nookie who had together recently won ITV talent show New Faces.

Bunny Baron made a return to the Lido in 1977 when he produced 'Take A Tripp 77' featuring Jack Tripp.

Bunny said at the time he believed the basic show formula hadn't changed a great deal in the 20 plus years since he was last in Cliftonville but modern audiences now expected better value for money with greater originality, colour and artistry – all influences of TV. People wanted a show to move swiftly along rather than be held up with sketches.

195. Photocall for the Lido Minstrel Show singers and dancers in 1980.

Mounting costs of hiring celebrities and a shrinking economy forced the management to look harder at the summer shows in the Lido Theatre. The main summer show style later changed in the late 1970s to end of the pier style entertainments under the titles of 'There'll Always Be An England' which met with reasonable success, as did 'The Al Jolson Minstrel Show' – a line up of now unfashionable black and white minstrels plus chorus girls. Hard work put in by the management and cast in 1978 paid off with a surge of seat sales for the theatre.

Wanting to win a younger audience to the centre, a new discotheque named Hades had been opened in August 1971. This was housed in the former dance cavern bar behind the theatre. Aimed strictly at the over 20s it was open in the summer from Thursday to Sunday between 9pm until 2am. Exotic dancers appeared on Thursday nights. A supper licence in the disco's restaurant saw doors actually open from 8pm. In the early 1980s, the name was changed to Colonel Bogey's, necessitated in part by an unwanted reputation for disorder.

196. Making finishing touches to Colonel Bogey's exterior.

197. A view of the Lido Sun Deck in 1947. Compare how little had changed with the photo below.

198. The Sun Deck in 1980 when music and competitions were led by organist Tony Savage.

A leisurely life at the Lido

199. The Old Time Music Hall line up for 1980 comprised these dancers and performers.

Out on the sun terrace organist Tony Savage entertained thousands of deck chaired holiday-makers every summer for many years, while the Jamaica Bar, restyled for £10,000 in 1973, saw the arrival of Norris Leslie playing a three manual, 10 rank Lowrey Citation organ. Both Norris and Tony would be working hard seven days a week at the season's height to entertain.

Nearby was the Olde Tyme Music Hall which had transferred in the late 1960s from Dreamland when Margate Estates sold out to Phonographic Equipment.

From 1970 the show was produced by and featured Al and Kathie Dene – 'Majestic Mancunians, masters of merriment and melody' – and their artistes. In 1973 their growing

200. Al Dene, Chairman of Old Time Music Hall in the 1970s.

201. The newly refurbished Jamaica Bar in 1973.

202. How the Lido pool looks these days. Just like an oversized sandpit.

203. The darker tarmac gives an idea of where the Lido Theatre once stood.

success and loyal following justified a £12,000 makeover of the Cliff Café into the music hall's new summer base. Al and Kathie ran these shows until the end of the decade but music hall continued here in one form or another until the Lido's closure at the end of the 1981 season.

In July of that year Associated Leisure announced in a short press statement it had sold the complex to Golden Coast Amusements of Ilfracombe.

Things didn't work out for the new owners and despite some ambitious plans to rebuild the swimming pool into something more modern and meeting new safety regulations, the Lido has been sold on more than once and has largely been dormant ever since. The theatre, beginning to show signs of age even in the early 1980s, has long since been demolished. Only a difference in the colour of the tarmac surface marks the site. The pool was filled in years ago to become little more than an oversized sandpit.

In that time various developers and Thanet District Council have wrangled over what to do with the place. Currently, a snooker club and bar still operate but it's fair to say the rest of the Lido is a sad blot on the local landscape, heightening the overall shabbiness of what was once a prosperous part of town.

Perhaps all is not lost. Back in August 2000, owner Neville Borck applied to the council to move the famous Lido beacon elsewhere in the complex and build a new block of flats, a 30 room hotel and leisure facilities in its place. Plans also included a health and beauty village, three restaurants, nightclub and a language school.

Outline planning permission was granted a few months later subject to an agreement between council and developer but this was not settled. As a result there has been little or no outward progress since – other than repainting and reglazing the beacon, which stands in the same spot, in summer 2003. Further development plans may be announced in early 2004.

204. The Lido beacon, seen here in 1980, still stands proud and was given a much needed repaint in 2003.

Acknowledgements

The author is indebted to the following for their help in the production of this book:

Isle of Thanet Gazette, Margate, for use of photographs numbered
122, 123, 136, 138, 139 and 148

Kent County Library, Margate, for use of photographs numbered 1 and 2

Margate Museum, Margate, for use of photographs numbered
26, 35, 38, 51, 61, 67, 70, 73, 80, 84, 87, 89, 98, 99, 100, 104, 108,
154, 167, 171, 176, 177, 183, 189 and 201.

Simmons Aerofilms Ltd, Potters Bar, for use of photograph number 79

Mr Vic McCoy, Birchington, for use of photograph number 65.

Please note all other photographs belong to the Bill Evans Collection and must
not be reproduced without prior reference to the author.

Mr Raymond Dolling, Harlow, for use of his feature material which
first appeared in Theatrephile magazine, June 1984,
and providing background information.

Mrs Susan Evans for her unstinting support throughout.